D0768447

Discovering
The Natural Laws
That Govern
The Universe

Discovering
The Natural Laws
That Govern
The Universe

Gaining Inner Awareness, Prosperity And Harmony

Ralph D. Jordan

Inner Perceptions, Inc.
Kailua-Kona, Hawaii

Cover and interior design by Pete Masterson, Æonix Publishing Group, www.aeonix.com

Copyright © 2001 Ralph D. Jordan. All rights reserved. No part of this book may be reproduced in any form or by any means, electronic or mechanical, including photocopying, recording, or by any information storage and retrieval system, without permission in writing from the copyright holder, except for the inclusion of brief quotations in a review.

ISBN: 0-9667683-1-0
LCCN: 00-110848

00 01 02   9 8 7 6 5 4 3 2 1

Published by:
Inner Perceptions, Inc.
P.O. Box 2652
Kailua-Kona, HI 96745
Phone/Fax: 808-325-5268
email: nich@gte.net
www.innerperceptions.com

Printed in the United States of America

Contents

Message from the Publisher

This book reflects the wisdom that Ralph Jordan has gained in more than 35 years of working with these natural laws as he has shared his understanding of their function and application with seekers from all walks of life.

The purpose of these collected teachings is to serve as a guide to building the bridge between man's laws and natural laws to enable the seeker to be in the world but not submerged by it, to create his world as he wishes to experience it.

It is the author's hope that this book will assist man to live a balanced life in the fulfillment of his purpose and mission on the earth plane, and that it may serve as a signpost to those who might temporarily feel lost on the road to self-recognition and self-awareness.

May it be a beacon of light to help the seeker to find the way through the sometimes stormy seas of life to the safe harbor of God's kingdom of love, wisdom and light.

May it be a road map that shows, not necessarily the easy way, but the responsible way of learning, being and expressing who man truly is as he travels the road of his evolution to his destination's end.

May he know that every step on the way that is taken with an open mind and an open heart with the intent to bring out the best in himself and others will bring him closer to his Father's home of many mansions.

May the love and light of this universal intelligence reign supreme and may man always know that it does.

I AM with you always.

Part One

Introduction to the Natural Laws

Oftentimes we wonder what laws govern all of our deeds and what disciplines we must put into action in order to be able to better understand the movement that is taking place in our atmosphere, in our private, social, family life, business life, and most of all in our spiritual life. Generally, we are looking for a rule of thumb that allows us to govern our actions so that we can enjoy all of the benefits that are promised and we see some people using so abundantly.

God gave us, through Moses, the Ten Commandments to follow. But there are laws that go beyond those Ten Commandments and beyond man's laws. We call these laws the natural laws or God's laws. These laws are energy frequencies that pervade the universe and are in effect at all times. They are immutable and unchangeable. They are a state of consciousness; an understanding that we put into our mind as a vision of our own identity, our own self, of what we've learned, of what we need to learn. The natural laws are an insight of what we are going to be as we begin to discover the universe that exists within us.

I refer to them as natural laws, but they are also called

cosmic laws, universal laws, esoteric laws, divine mind's laws, universal intelligence laws, God's laws.

The natural laws, though they have labels and identifications, really represent the many facets of consciousness that we vacillate in in our moment-to-moment quests and situations. They are that state of understanding that we achieve as we look at the experiences that we encounter in life and understand the lessons that each experience teaches us. They are moving in us, through us and around us. The natural laws do not relieve us of our personal responsibility to ourselves and our evolution.

They are energies that crisscross our globe and emanate their presence through our atmosphere. When we try to visualize the globe as a sphere with all of these laws crisscrossing around it, ultimately we will get a symbol that looks something like the atom. When we are in conjunction with the natural laws we are creating an atmosphere of harmony. When we are not, we are creating an atmosphere of static. Static brings distortion within our comprehensive abilities and doesn't allow us to see clearly that which is the growth or the story that is being relayed to us. It doesn't allow us to formulate a clear picture of our own self, our own purpose and our own cause for being here on this earth plane.

Our perception, our discipline and our obedience are the factors that determine whether these laws work for us or against us. It is not enough to just intellectually know them. We have to put them into action. We are the master and captain of all the laws; we must learn to control them. We don't want to make the laws just disciplinary practices; we want the laws to become an integrated way of life for us.

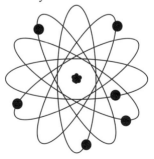

What are laws?

What is man's definition of a law? Let's see what the dictionary has to say.

From the *Webster's Encyclopedic Unabridged Dictionary of the English Language:*

1. The principles and regulations established by a government and applicable to a people whether in the form of legislation or of custom and policies recognized and enforced by judicial decision.
2. Any written or positive rule or collection of rules prescribed under the authority of the state or nation, as by the people in its constitution.
3. A divinely appointed order or system.
4. A commandment or a revelation from God.

What is man's definition of natural law?

1. A principle or body of laws considered as derived from nature, right reason or religion and as ethically binding in human society.

We all know that man's laws are constituted so that we might live in harmony with our fellow man and continue to pursue our evolutionary processes through life. Then there are God's laws or natural laws. It would be most beneficial for man to adhere to natural laws because they are continuous and eternal. Man's laws change from time to time, from government to government and from people to people. In order to be able to live in conjunction with man's laws, we must really learn to understand and put into practice God's laws.

Most of us have been brought up to believe that the only laws that God left us were the Ten Commandments, which have been greatly misunderstood and certainly not followed. Now we will be learning about laws that govern the influences of our planet and atmosphere that go beyond those Ten Commandments and beyond man's laws. The Ten Commandments are man's interpretation of God's laws. They are the basis that allows us to become more aware and disciplined to more constructively use the natural laws that are continuously in effect within the universe. Natural law is immutable; natural law just is. The Ten Commandments, which were man's interpretation of the steps that would allow man to live cohesively with the natural laws, can be altered according to a society, a religious faction, a philosophical faction.

If man's law and natural law are not coexisting very well, as can be represented by the scales of justice, if they are not balanced, then in some respect we have misunderstood or have refused to be obedient to the laws that are permanent.

Natural laws/man's laws—their function in our life

The natural laws govern prosperity and the awakening of the inner being. They allow us to see ourselves as we really are. I believe that all mankind is on a quest to ultimately see itself in its true form, its true identity. We adhere to certain laws of man in an attempt to use those laws to bring us to a place where we find our own identity, our own purpose and direction in life. I believe that each of us is looking for a direction in life. I believe we are attempting to create a bridge between the law of societal comprehension and the law of divine awareness. We take the laws of societal comprehension, and we use them to build a bridge so that we might experience the law of divine comprehension. Together we have the ascended quality that allows us to work in this densified plane, yet enables us, if we believe in past lives, to recognize the influences that we have acquired from past lives, then to utilize that understanding and awareness that we have derived from our past sojourns on this earth plane.

How do we use God's laws to work through karmic influences and become more aware of our dharmic influences?

Few of us understand the magnitude of the natural laws at work in our daily lives. Even those of us who have learned to use them, speak about them, question them, ignore them and do not obey them. The laws are the creative energy of divine mind that knows nothing, sees nothing and hears nothing but the perfection of the laws through its created images in being. The laws sustain life, evolution and ascent into the vistas of astral, etheric, causal and atmospheric planes. It is not the misuse of the laws that creates pain, misery and degradation, it is the ignorance of them. But ignorance of the laws doesn't excuse us from them.

We move through society always attempting to meet the expectations of our karmic family and our karmic society, of our educational facilities and situations. We evaluate our adherence to societal law by the successes we see manifested and we are able to demonstrate.

Such as, in adherence to societal law, a man may become an engineer and he can meet the expectations of all those experts in that societal concept who accept themselves as engineers. This allows him to build the bridge so that he might see himself as a caretaker. Over the years, I have begun to realize that I am really not quite more than a caretaker. Because my students are God's property, this church is God's property, this wisdom, universal as it might be, is God's property; I have become a caretaker of God's property. So I have followed the laws of man, acquainted myself with the laws of cosmic or God intelligence, and then have chosen, as a teacher, to be a caretaker of God's property.

According to society, genealogy confers upon us the knowledge that we are a product of the genes and of the emotional and mental influences of our parents as we are birthed into physical existence. Then we are a product of our family, educational, religious and ethnic backgrounds, all of which are the exemplification of man's laws. But we are also a product of a greater parent, and that parent is the administrator, creator and author of the natural, evolutionary course of society, of mankind. We attempt not only to understand, accept and obey man's laws, but we also attempt to incorporate God's laws.

The first step we take is to acquaint ourselves intellectually with the natural laws that constantly pervade our atmosphere. Then we attempt to work in conjunction with man's laws. Note the key word—in conjunction.

Balancing man's law with natural law

The natural laws help us to be much more accurate in our analysis of what takes place on a day-to-day basis in our lives because we can see it as physical expression. That's what life is all about. Life is the densified, physical expression of where we have been out of balance in our application of not only man's laws but also natural laws.

I am going to acquaint you a little more with natural law and how one uses it in order to balance man's law. This is quite important because many of us have suffered under this imbalance of the laws, and our lives express the suffering manifested through the imbalance in utilizing these two sets of laws. Carl Gustav Jung asked each of his students to keep a journal. They would put down on paper their comprehension, understanding, utilization and application of those two great commodities: natural law and man's law. They were then able to understand where they had not totally comprehended themselves and where they had limited themselves. This practice assisted his students in eradicating their limitations and allowing them to be.

Being in balance with the natural laws means we know we are.

For example I say to this gentleman: "You are very wealthy, and I want $1,000 from you. I want to use it for God's purpose." If he has gone through the comprehension and the study of positive thinking, speaking and viewing, then he should know that he is infinitely wealthy and able to give $1,000 to be utilized for the furtherance of the education and for the awakening of all of God's children to those two concepts: natural law/man's law. How we discern for ourselves is in the recognition of the obstacles that we create in our minds that prohibit us from being able to use our wealth willingly, not because it's being forced from us, not because it's being demanded, but because we know we are.

When I am doing blindfold billets I actually present a challenge. I am demonstrating an ability. That is what producing phenomena is all about. It is the demonstration of an ability not solely owned by one person, and that can be demonstrated by anyone who is in conjunction with or in balance with natural law and man's law.

I want you to not just learn what the natural laws are, I want you to also see how in conjunction with societal, karmic and personality identity you don't create the bridge to natural law. You are not standing in the middle, being able to express something to the world. I want that point to become absolutely and totally visual in your heads. Envision the scales, with man's laws on one side and natural laws on the other side. We live in a physical body and we can transmute anything by becoming aware of natural laws. We can use the natural laws as an influence as we obey man's laws. We can each then become a pillar of light by bringing the two scales (of justice) into balance.

If we are totally tied into man's law, the scale will weigh down and attract whatever is in the atmosphere. If we are totally tied into natural law, the scale will weigh down and release everything that is in it. When we bring the scales into balance, they send out an energy that creates the vortex, with which we are then totally in balance.

For example: When a man denies he is a healer, when I as the teacher, as the expression, the living energy of God's concept tell him he is, then he must look at his own stagnation and limitations. Suppose I see that he has created this bridge and he has brought a balance between all that he is beyond the illusion of what he judges and evaluates himself to be. Then, if he wishes to put into action all the laws, he is faced with the concept of obedience. It is obedience to a philosophy, an educational system, to the very projection and understanding of what is being revealed to him, because nothing will ever become a truth to him until he uses it. It will always be a thesis. But yet, that God part of him, those genes that were instilled in him by Father/Mother God, demand that he recognize them, bring them out and utilize them so that he can be in balance with man's laws and natural laws.

Why would we look at a living energy of God's concept, at a symbol of power, at a teacher, and not know that we have the identical power, unless we are dealing with our own judgment and comparison? Why would we compare ourselves with anyone else?

To my students: Try to see yourselves as I see you. It will show you where you have limited yourselves. I say this man is a fantastic healer, because that's how I see him. Now he has to evaluate how to heal himself. That will show him where he is out of harmony with natural laws and man's laws.

It has been so easy for me to give you certain insights because I think and see you as being wealthy. And, under certain conditions, you accept that concept from natural law and you allow it to work in your life. So what happens is, it throws away your intellectual mind because I thought and proclaimed it. You allowed it to work, and it manifested. You have to put into action the concept of release.

The only way a person can ever be able to get over his feelings and his self-created negative belief structure is by recognizing them and asking himself if he chooses to live under them. That is why the student professes complete and total obedience so that he might think, feel, and create in the form of the person or being whom he has chosen to be the illuminating factor to his malfunctions. Thus, we have the medium because the medium in his ethic and in his sense of balance between the natural laws and man's laws, and in his natural sense of comprehension of his identity, acts as the illuminating factor that shows the seeker where he is unbalanced between the natural laws and man's laws, and where he is being limited by them. I have taught that a symbol (a medium) is a representation of an ability, and the genius of that ability is determined by the balance between man's laws and natural laws. Unfortunately, many of us are limited by man's laws. We compare ourselves and we judge ourselves; we evaluate ourselves by man's laws, and with man's laws come expectations along the way.

Every book of philosophy and of religious understanding tells you that you are children of God, and in the New Testament, Jesus, who became the Christ, said:

> *Knock, and the door will be opened*
> *Seek, and ye shall find*
> *Ask, and it will be given unto you*

How can you knock, seek or ask if you are all tied up in man's laws?

For example: How can you resist my love? How can you classify it, label it, categorize it, and identify it? All you have to do is to open the door to experience it. When you don't experience it you have tied yourself into man's laws. That's why you come to classes and seminars, because it ignites within you your own awareness of your Godself, and you bask in it, but you also get caught in man's laws. Yet it is there for you, isn't it?

Must we abide by man's laws?

We must learn to look at man's laws and to abide by them. When we willfully choose to break them, we must know why we are breaking them and what purpose it serves. My great teacher told me long ago that it was my responsibility to live in the world. Do you know what living in the world means? It means that you collectively see what the world is, know that you have assisted in its being, and choose not to be submerged by the world.

If we break man's laws, we know the end result before each action we take because we create it. We prejudge and pre-work with it and manifest it just exactly as we want it.

Criminology has proven that the greatest percentage of criminals leave behind the tell tale sign that will ultimately lead them to being captured and punished because they know that they are breaking man's laws, and that in breaking man's laws they are breaking the natural laws.

Each of us in our own consciousness asks to be caught, to be punished, and we elect our associates, families, and companions to exemplify that punishment.

Natural laws covered in this book

The Law of Love

"Love ye one another as I have loved you." It is the *law of love*, and love begins with the self.

We love ourselves because we are. We love people because they are.

The *law of love* is designed to teach us the many facets of emotional, mental and physical distraction. When love is in action there is no comparison, no judgment, no disharmony, no lack. We love people even if it doesn't bring us any physical, mental or emotional gratification.

The Law of Compensation

We will be compensated in like measure for all the things that we do. Compensation is visual through the physical manifestations and the experiences that we encounter in this life.

It registers our attitude about ourselves, it registers our actions, and it shows us in the physical dimension all of those unrecognized, not understood and buried attitudes of ourselves that we are emanating into the ethers.

The *law of compensation* guarantees us that no one is going to get away with anything, even though it may appear that some people get away with mayhem, murder, injustices, misuse in this lifetime. The perpetrators of unbalanced actions will be compensated for them.

The Law of Cause and Effect

(Also called the law of karma and dharma, law of action and reaction and law of retribution.)

There is an underlying cause for every effect. A cause is

always a reflection of being in harmony with or an abuse of natural laws. A cause needs to be looked at and dealt with so that one can start the process of redirection through understanding when there is an out of balance effect.

The law of "As Above so Below and as Below so Above"

(Hereinafter called: law of "as above so below")

The *law of "as above so below"* is indicative of all the thoughts we project into the astral plane. These thoughts act as a magnet attracting, according to the *law of attraction,* like thoughts of the same dimensions and degrees, until they become solidified into experiences. Just as our balanced thoughts will attract balanced experiences, our disjointed and unbalanced thoughts will attract unbalanced experiences.

The Law of Attraction

To have love we must be love, to have truth we must be truth because like attracts like.

According to the *law of attraction* we attract individuals to us who reflect back to us what we've been, what we are or what we will be.

Like energies merge, like energies support each other, like energies are soul mates. Opposites create friction and grow from friction.

The Law of Divine Order

There is no right, there is no wrong, there just is.

Things are in divine order, they are in the order that we have created them, and we are in a sense divinity. All things are because they are meant to be, and there is good that will come out of all that transpires in the physical dimension.

My prayer: All things prophesied and predicted this day, oh God, please allow them to be done in accordance with thy will and not mine. Bless each of those who I have met today, open their hearts that they might see themselves in perfection as they are and always shall be. Protect them and guide them in accordance with divine order.

The Law of "It Matters Not"

It matters not what others think about us, it matters that we fulfill our mission and our purpose. It matters not how people react to us, it matters that we follow the natural laws.

The Law of Harmony

When we are in harmony with the world then we are not resistant to our creations.

The Law of Harmlessness

Who should we be the most harmless to? Certainly not to a critter, certainly not to another human being, but certainly to ourselves. We are so harmful to ourselves because we put ourselves in situations of stress, limitation, poverty and inadequacies.

The Law of Non-judgment

Judge not (others or yourself), that ye be not judged. For with what judgment you judge, ye shall be judged: and with what measures ye mete, it shall be measured to you again. Matthew 7: 1, 2.

Anything that we judge, fear, or allow to have importance in our life, we are going to have to experience.

The Law of Non-comparison

We are all created equal. We are the extensions of this divine consciousness.

If we compare ourselves to the rich man and his gift, then we have lost the purpose of giving. But if the penny is our all, it is as valuable as the rich man's gift.

The Law of Non-force

God's will be done, not mine.

We do not force our will on others. We do not bend people to our will. We do not force situations, decisions, statements, answers, etc. We also do not force ourselves into molds of other people's expectations. Non-force begins with us.

Part Two

Man's Law says—
Natural Law says—

Natural law does not demand that we obey it, it just says that we will pay the price if we don't. Man's law says, "We'll kill you if you don't obey. We'll reject you and throw you out of society if you don't obey." I do not think that we, as teachers and potential teachers, can be limited by man's law. If we were to begin by making a practice of attempting to obey man's law, making the bridge into natural law, we would find that there is no necessity to obey man's law, because we would be obeying natural law.

I am God: where is the division? Where is the separation? The division and separation only come when I start following and obeying man's laws. If I am following the natural laws, then I am the living expression of that energy that we call God, divine mind and consciousness. When I am not allowing that energy to flow through me because I am meeting someone else's expectations, then I have just turned my power to man's laws. The bridge is not seeing separation.

Man's laws and natural laws both exist; they reflect our karmic and dharmic responsibility. Man's laws reflect our karma;

the natural laws reflect our dharma. Natural law says there is no color or creed, we are wealthy, beautiful, and successful; the expression of the creative force that made us. Man's law says, "Now, wait a minute. You don't have a Ph.D. You aren't beautiful and you are too fat. You are too old to learn anything new." But when we get older and we finally find out we are not too old to learn something new, we can be overwhelmed by all that we can possibly achieve. Man's law says, "You are a woman, you have to get married. You have to go out and win someone's affection, and that someone has to prove you to you. He must sacrifice his whole life in total adoration to your glorious youthful beauty." Man's law also says: "If you get past 30, you have become an old maid."

Natural law says we are perfect, we can do anything, we are wealthy, we are healthy. When the realities of life say we are not, we need to look, not to society, but to ourselves. When we sacrifice our innate good, which is the exemplification and application of natural law, to comply with man's law, then I am afraid somewhere we are out of balance. Isn't it wonderful that we have all of these symbols going around in these physical vehicles that continuously reflect back to us the things we are? I have always found in building the bridge from natural law that the particular expression of man's law doesn't matter if I can simply go ahead and be comfortable with what I am doing, how I am doing it, and know that I am doing it for myself.

A lot of this natural law is just following our hearts, but unfortunately many of us do not use our hearts.

These are simple truths. We don't escape the necessity to bring the two scales into balance and to become the middle pillar. Balancing the scales is a recognition of our dark and light side and of actually coming into control. We all want to be the master of our own destiny, don't we? We achieve mastery through following the examples that ignite within us a greater awareness of what we are, who we are, and where we are going. So we either choose to indulge in the recognition of that darker self, which can be equated to man's laws, or we can see the light side of ourselves, which can be equated to the natural laws.

How Do We Buy Into Man's Laws? —Examples

The best way to balance karma is through understanding, not through sacrifice or self-denial. What
helps us to understand it? Isn't balancing any karma
being good to ourselves? Isn't it coming to that place
of divine recognition?

Are you being good to yourself by man's law or natural law?
Only you can make the discernment and the choice. When
you buy into man's law you don't know that you are loved
already, and you are still looking for outside circumstances to
prove it to you. I happen to think you are love and I find it
very difficult to understand why you have such difficulty in
expressing it. Perhaps it is because you have bought into man's
law, and you don't believe you are love anyway. You are these
laws I am talking about.

Karma is only an educational factor that helps us to understand ourselves. That's why we reproduce it, recreate it and
continue to foster it all through this particular life's endeavors.
We refuse to make that bridge between the natural law and
man's law and be in the middle.

Let me give you a little test that shows how you buy into

man's law. Would you stand up, young lady? Would you stand up, young man? Look at each other and meet yourself, because everything negative or positive that you evaluate or judge about another person is a reflection of you. Everything that you see and like in the other person you have accepted in yourself. Everything you see and you don't like in the other person you are failing to recognize in yourself. That's how you can meet yourselves in your various degrees of acceptance, recognition and application of the laws. You would say according to man's law, "But she is a woman and he is a man." Untrue. They are existing energy. That is what Carl Gustav Jung taught us about the yin and yang. That's how we break the natural laws. We don't see from a recognizing standpoint the various evolutions that are reflections of our own evolution as a part of our education. How we discern that is in our attitude of thought and discernment. You want self-awareness, a bridge between man's law and natural law? That's your beginning step.

Man's law assists us in creating our personality, which is formed by all of man's expectations, all the things that we willingly put ourselves into and subject ourselves to because we are unaware of ourselves.

Let's take an example: We have been educated to apply the *law of harmlessness* in such an unbalanced way; not to harm others but to be harmful to ourselves because we are educated, again through our choices, not to be selfish or egotistic. In order to be accepted by society we must deny the self, and we call it humility. We are afraid that if we were to recognize the many facets of the self and not cover the self with a lot of encrustation that we would not be accepted in society. So we live an illusion of harmfulness to ourselves. Unfortunately, when we are harmful to ourselves we are extremely harmful to society, because we present illusions as facts for society to base its concepts, its identities, its wishes and hopes on.

Then at a point in time when it pleases us or we feel safe and comfortable, we pull off all of this illusion and face individuals with our real self. Then we do more destruction than if we had shown them our real self from the beginning. All the role playing has hurt us, yes, but think of the delusion that other individuals have lived under, because we have promoted this illusion for acceptance and manipulative control. Now we are yanking it away from them and we are leaving them open and bleeding because they had founded their life structure or their identity on the illusion that we presented to them.

In all this discipline of being harmless at the cost of being harmful to ourselves, which is illusion, we will only be more harmful when we are faced with situations we call life and death. The adrenaline that is pumped through our body at that moment of life or death, causing us to respond without calculation for self-preservation, will supersede like a power surge all the illusionary disciplines, and we will do everything to survive. You would be surprised how frequently we are threatened in life and death situations and how we respond in an instant with a war like attitude when our comfortable concept of ourselves is threatened by information. The superficial obedience to harmlessness is actually very harmful.

I don't break the laws because I don't want to pay the price for it. So I am being harmless to myself. It has nothing to do with you, it has everything to do with me. But I am honest enough to admit it and let you calculate your own vision. I don't profess to be "holier than thou" because you might find that I have feet of clay, and then I would have broken the *law of harmlessness* because you trusted me to be perfect; you wanted me to be perfect. But then I would be harmful to myself if I fostered that illusion because if I would allow you to continue to create that illusion I might have to deal with cause and effect and look at my reason for allowing you to create that illusion: what manipulative power do I want to have over you and what do I want to gain from you that I don't think I am entitled to? The effect would be destructive to my own sense of identity, especially if you were stingy and poverty-conscious and refused to give me what I thought I wanted from you. Then I would constantly have to try harder.

Apply the same concept to love and see how often we do that to get love. This is very harmful to ourselves because we let somebody see an illusion of what we sense they expect from us, what they want us to be for them, and then we try being it for a while. If they are suffering from poverty consciousness, and they don't give us what we want, then we create an illusionary concept of ourselves. We either try harder or we project a great deal of anger, and we enter into strife, criticism, judgment, denial, which is all self-destructive. Look at all the laws we have broken.

Let's say a psychic desires to give psychic messages to an audience. If he is concerned about impressing everybody, then he has bought into man's laws and has ignored natural laws.

People who sell themselves for the titillation of a physical gratification have bought into man's laws and are certainly not involved in natural laws, because natural law says that they have everything. That's why learned individuals, such as Dr. Jon Speller, have written books about the seed money practice, but you have to put that into action by building the bridge from the realization that you have everything.

When we know we have something we stop judging ourselves to prove it. When we know we have love we are free to use our talents to produce all the rest of the symbols before us. It is the struggle with man's law that keeps us constantly denying ourselves, constantly being unkind to ourselves, constantly making ourselves ill because we don't know we are wealthy. All God is asking us for is that we use our talents trustingly. It has always been simple. All of Christ's, Buddha's and Krishna's teachings are so simple that we have to make a big production out of them. We must look at the situation, see where we have bought into man's law, know the natural laws, and then stop judging and comparing ourselves.

When we are attempting to build a bridge between man's law and natural law, we are as qualified and capable as any other human being. The reason that we have the symbols of individuals who have become successful is so we will continue to deal with our self-doubts and our own self-evaluations. We can achieve what is being demonstrated to us. The reason for phenomena is for us to see and to end up believing and recognizing that there is life after death and that it isn't just this particular lifetime, that there is more. So when we start thinking that we can borrow money from another person, we are buying into our own particular concept of man's law. If we are asked to stretch into a broader consciousness by any particular person whom we have recognized as the symbol of what we are, then we are required to do the stretching, not to look for someone to do it for us.

Many experiences in our lives show us where we are not in solid conjunction with these two pillars of existing energy (man's law/natural law), where we aren't building that bridge between them and standing in the middle. You would be surprised how few of us, when we look at a situation we have created for ourselves, actually ever accept the responsibility for it. We say to ourselves, "It's somebody else's fault; it's my wife's fault, my husband's fault, my boyfriend's fault," and all that sort of thing, but ultimately, it really, actually is our fault.

We do the same thing with our karma. I have heard so many people say, "It's my karma to experience this pain or this particular limitation." That is absolutely and completely untrue. It's your karma to recognize where you are out of balance, and then to take the necessary steps to get yourself out of it and become balanced in your expression on the earth plane.

We do let others influence our opinion and our concept of ourselves. Every thought we project that limits us is what we need to work with. We need to say, "I am, I can, I will."

Give that power to yourself. Look at your situation, recognize where you bought into man's law and where you have ignored natural law, and you will be able to discipline yourself. Isn't that what you are doing now by reading this book? You have to understand that everything in your life is what you've created. Know that you have done it, and sit back and say, "Okay, I bought into man's law here, I bought into natural law here," and then say to yourself, "Where do I take it from here?" Natural law is always there for you, yet it requires discipline. That's why I require obedience and submission from my students, because we have been controlled for so long by man's law, we are not ready to listen to natural law. That does not mean that we abort man's law, it means we try to obey it. That's the 50-50 we give to society. We try to obey man's law so that we can obey natural law. We cannot justify our disobedience to man's law. If we are being disobedient to man's laws we have to pay the price. When we are disobedient to natural law we can't avoid paying a price (and it's called karma), but we can understand it. And once we understand it we can control it. It is only the things that we don't understand, that we feel manipulated by that we can't control, and they frighten us. So when we are dealing with the laws, we must come to a place where we have ourselves so in control that we are able to understand the *law of non-judgment,* because we can't break the law that we have created for ourselves. Let go and let God.

When the student ultimately reaches a point where he feels as though he knows nothing and has nothing, he is in the most perfect, balanced state because he has experienced that influence between man's law and natural law. That's when he is ready to make a choice. That's the precipice: it is formless, shapeless, we don't have any guarantee, we don't have anything concrete that we can judge it by. We have to submit to it because we simply have to go for it. It is as though we know what we want, but we don't know we can get it. Once we have committed ourselves to it, then all the things that keep us from having it are our karma. It is our refusal to work with natural laws that prevents us from "having it all." It is being willing to submit ourselves to a higher concept. We do not ask to be given what we already have. We ask for assistance to bring it out.

When I say to you, "Look at your houses, are you happy with them?" and you answer "No" then you have to say to yourselves, "Where have I not put in my full efforts?" All the reasons that you give yourselves as to why you haven't put your efforts into the very things that will keep you in conjunction with natural law keep you tied into man's law. That's all I am asking you to look at. That's what tells you what you are limiting yourselves by.

When you suddenly recognize that you don't fit in at work, with your family, etc., you have already walked away from the natural law, you already are in man's law. You are judging the people with whom you are working and comparing yourself to them. You wouldn't be there if there weren't a purpose to be served. So, when we work with the *law of non-judgment*, we must sit back and say: I am here for a purpose. I have chosen this situation. How I can best serve this purpose and get on with my growth and evolution is through learning from the individuals I am exposed to. You have already broken the law when you start entering into judgment.

But you do have the right to discern. You can sit back and look at what is going on around you, and you can decide if you want it to be a part of your expression. The minute you start condemning the expression of other people you have gotten right back in the middle of it, and you have lessened your own abilities to act as the teacher and to free yourself from the indebtedness. You have forgotten the *law of divine order*. You chose the experience for a lesson. It is there for you to see yourself as you really are. What else would be the purpose of you being in the experience? You are all God in action.

We can look at life and society and we can see where we have failed to recognize that we are God in action. We have bought into man's law instead of natural law and natural law says we are, and if we are, then there are no limitations. Why would we need someone to prove to us that we are? When we deal with other people, we are actually judging and comparing according to what we feel we haven't done in order to fulfill our own particular purpose and mission. That is the whole thing about gossip, judgment, ridicule. If I discern that I don't want to be a part of something I don't have to walk away from it, I can simply shut down. It can go around about me, but I can still be what I am.

We will know that a particular experience is fulfilled when we can leave it without the slightest feeling of disappointment. We will love that situation and know that it just does not happen to be a situation that is constructive for us. When we judge a situation we are a part of it. When we judge co-workers, acquaintances, friends and family we are doing the same thing that we are judging. It's just that we haven't seen it as prevalent in our character. So we are out of conjunction with the *law of non-judgment* because we are not supposed to judge. We are supposed to understand the karmic influences and know that each individual has the innate right to choose whatever he or she wishes to be, and we cannot force him or her to be otherwise.

Individual Laws in Action – Examples

Love

The *law of love* reveals that we've got to have a wild, wonderful love affair with ourselves. But then someone might say that we are narcissistic or egotistic. So we couldn't possibly have a love affair with ourselves because we are educated to believe we should do absolutely anything except love ourselves. Our education says we must sacrifice ourselves, first to our family, then to our profession, our society, our religion, our culture and to our country. So we can't love ourselves. That's why there are so many illnesses, because people are not balanced in practicing this *law of love*. We direct love to everyone else, while very humbly saying, "I'm not sure you should love me because I'm totally unworthy." And God help us when we respond by not loving them! This *law of love* really requires that we start loving ourselves, even if we have created a cancer for ourselves.

If we are in conjunction with this *law of love*, then we will stop fearing this cancer and start loving it. Then we can begin to see it not as a life taker but as a life opportunity for greater self-recognition. When we start loving instead of judging and encapsulating the situations that we encounter in our environments because we made them and we see them as opportunities to learn about ourselves, we will be able to rebalance them, heal them and stop intensifying them.

We must learn to love these negative parts of us. We must give them a constructive direction and not fear them or deny them. These negative aspects, our illnesses, are like our kids and we really can't deny our kids. They are constantly there showing us everything that we have done and even accusing us of doing more than what we have done. But we still have to love them. We haven't been a victim; no one has done it to us; we have manifested it, created it either in this lifetime or in another, and it is a learning opportunity. With both our illnesses and our kids we really have to love them and listen to what they are saying.

It's so easy to love those people who flatter us, who seem to gratify our every desire. But our Christ demonstrated a love that was far deeper because he loved his Judas while his Judas betrayed him. If we would simply surround ourselves with those people who think like we think, we would be a sect, we would truly be inviting self-destruction. But can we love, will we love, those people who think differently, who cause us to go deeper into our reserves of determination, self-will, self-motivation and self-expansion? That's what we are going to encounter and that's what we are afraid of. We are afraid to take ourselves by the bootstraps and direct ourselves through the application of non-judgment towards ourselves. When I push a button in you and point out one of your characteristics I already know that that same characteristic exists within me. But it is up to me to let it rear its head or to discipline and control it.

We can sit back and fill this mind with thesis, but it is a thesis until it is applied, until it is demonstrated. I don't care how much we think we know. So don't speak of love, show me.

We must ask ourselves what we don't like about the characteristics of others, what they are showing us. We have done one of three things. We have hidden them from ourselves, which means we have denied them. Or, we have recognized them and are covering them over with a lot of self-discipline and illusion. Or, we have recognized them and worked through them. If we have worked through them, then we can accept them. We won't like them in the actions and reactions of another person, but we know that they will eventually produce growth. That's the basis of remaining in conjunction with the laws. I do not have to like what is happening in the world, but I do have to love the world because it provides me an opportunity for expression. I can go about the country teaching and sharing what I know works.

Loving is very easy when we are able to see the God relationship and to discern that since God is in all things, all things deserve love. We cannot always be the disciplinarian who gives and takes according to an individual's accepted performances. Love, once it is given can never be taken away. Like and acceptance come and go, but love is such a vital essence that once we have given it, we can't extract it. We can deny like, association, approval, but we can't take away love once we have given it. We can't even take it away from ourselves, once we have given it. The idea is to give it.

Love is that fluid that cleans away all the cobwebs. It is that pure water that flows through our being and quenches all of our cells' thirst. It is the air that we breathe; it is the scent that we smell; it is the sun in the sky as it warms our body; it is the bird that causes us to know that we too can fly. It is the cloud that reminds us of what we are; it is the star at night that leads our way; it is that simple feeling that today we are okay. That is love.

Love is waking up in the morning, happy to be alive, saying: "This is God's day and I am going to be his instrument this day." It is looking out and seeing a storm and the rain beating down and from within your heart being able to say: "Look at all this glorious liquid sunshine. I want to go out into the rain and just take it all in, permeate my clothes, my skin, everything." It is knowing that being in that liquid sunshine is going to wash away all your cares. It is like taking a fishing rod and baiting it very tenderly and getting in your boat and casting it into the stream, and as the anchor and the hook go into the water watching the ripples and seeing the ripples as symbols of life and listening to the birds twitter and knowing that the sun is going to rise and that everything is well with the world. That is love.

Today, we woke up, and we took our first breath. We've got a whole day in which to make everything beautiful if we just love ourselves.

Seeker: What frequency does the *law of love* work on?

Jordan: The *law of love* works on all of the frequencies. We have to love all the situations we have put ourselves into because they are a creation of our own making. The only way we can understand situations is by loving them and not fearing them.

The more we fear a thing, the more we are employing ignorance. The more we judge a thing, the more we are employing just knowledge. But we are supposed to be employing wisdom in all the things we immerse ourselves in, so we also have to employ love. Non-judgment also vacillates on all different energy patterns. It is our job to increase the velocity of that energy.

We can define which energy pattern a law works on, but that is only knowledge. Wisdom comes from the realization that if we are vacillating at a denser frequency, we must uplift our whole vibratory field. These laws then have to be implanted in the vibratory field that we are creating for ourselves. But we have to be able to vacillate on all those levels. It is not enough to know on what level what energy works. The ultimate task for all of us is to take whatever energy pattern we need at that point in time and infuse it with an energy pattern we are creating. What is the value of defining what the energy patterns are? There is no great value other than keeping our intellect busy. The basic simple truth is the fact that whatever energy level any law works on, we have to employ that energy level into what we are creating.

Seeker: What is love?

Jordan: Light Of Vital Energy. When it is vital it is living. Energy is totally dead when it becomes encapsulated, when you break the *law of non-judgment* and you judge one another, when you encapsulate and limit one another. Love is expressing energy; love is being energy; love is vital. Love is the essence that all people are looking for because they are stagnated in their own compared personalities, in their own judgment. My teacher said, "Whatever you judge in life, you will have to experience." Believe me that is 100 percent true. Everything you judge, you will experience. Everything you abhor, you will be. What you see in others is a reflection of your own being.

So when you see someone who truly loves himself, it is a reflection of your own being. There has never been a person who successfully demonstrates the *law of love* in action who didn't first see it in action elsewhere.

There has never been a successful businessman who didn't first see a successful businessman elsewhere and then decided that he could be one, too.

Now I have just given you a little secret on how to bring about your own better expressions of phenomena. When you see something in others, it can become predominant in you because you associate with it. What you associate with is what you absorb and ultimately begin to see in yourself. I would only associate with successful metaphysicians because I know the *law of attraction*. When I see it in you, then obviously it must be in me. If I see less than love in you, then I see less than love in me.

Remember some of your unguarded thoughts of comparison and judgment that you have had about your friends, your relationships, etc. Can you see how you've experienced what you've judged? Just look at the labels you put on one another. Don't you know that you are going to be those labels? To say, "I am sorry," is not enough, because the only thing you are sorry about is that you got caught. If you were sorry, you wouldn't have done it in the first place. So you change it by understanding and knowing why you did it. Again, where do you find love?

Seeker: In a flower.

Jordan: Yes, the flower loves itself. You can see it there, but that doesn't necessarily mean you've got it. You can find it in the guru, too, but that doesn't mean that you have it. You can find it in poetry, but that means that the pages of the book have it, that doesn't mean you have it. So where are you going to find love? You find it inside of you, that's the only place to find it. You can't ask another person for it because that means they've got it and you have to beg for it. Love is **Light Of Vital Energy**, and you might as well give that to yourself and have an abundance of its creating, manifesting energy flowing to you, from within you like a river.

In almost all of the difficult clinical cases of every known disease the victim will respond to love. The most difficult cases of self-abuse through self-judgment, self-criticism, self-comparison, self-denial will respond to love. Our method of healing with all of our psychological innovations and our psychiatric treatments will only produce a greater self-awareness through guidance, love, understanding, acceptance and encouragement.

It's too bad we don't employ it with ourselves. We can do it for someone else, but when it comes to taking the simple truth and applying it on a moment-to-moment basis, we want to judge ourselves as inadequate and unworthy, and we want to tell love how to respond to us. We will even close our eyes to love when we see it and it doesn't fit our demands. We would rather have someone prove their love for us by lying to us instead of experiencing their love because they tell us the truth. It takes more love to tell the truth than to create lies to pacify your needs.

Show me someone who will tell me the truth and I will show you someone who is loving because he is ready and willing to endure the aftermath and the projection of very harmful criticism and judgment. Love, where will we find it? We will find it the same place we will find God, Christ, Lao-tse, Babaji, the same place we'll find all of the ascended ones—mostly inside ourselves. When we can see the light in us, we can see the light in someone else.

Seeker: You said we have to love people but don't have to like their actions. For me love is a voluntary action. If it's something I have to do, it's not love.

Jordan: To like is voluntary. Love is.

Seeker: If love is, then it is. I don't have to make a special effort to love.

Jordan: Yes, love is. Then tell me why you don't love yourself. Yes, you have love, and the only being you have to love is you. Once you give love to yourself, it can never be taken away. You have it permanently and you have your Christ identity, your Godself. As long as you confuse loving with liking, your Godself and your Christed being will be the yo-yo that springs in and out according to your performances and your acceptance of those performances.

Yes, you have to give love to the most difficult person of all, yourself. You don't have to give love to me because I've already got it. You can share love with me when you've got it. But if you haven't got it, you can't expect me to give my love away. You have to give it to yourself, or you won't have anything to share. That happens to be that natural law in action. Until you give it to yourself, you only have acceptance, like, expectations and titillation to share, but not love.

And it isn't giving love in degrees according to your liking of yourself; it is in giving love to every aspect of yourself because every aspect serves a purpose.

The affirmation is, "I love my toes because they

allow me to stand and fulfill God's purposes. I love my feet because they allow me to walk God's pathway. I love my ankles because they join me to my calves and allow me to fulfill God's purposes. I love my knees because they allow me to be flexible," and so forth. I don't like it when my hands rebel, when my feet become lazy, when my mind becomes concrete. But I love them. I can change what I don't like, but I can't produce love where there isn't any. You have nothing to give until you've got love. We can hope to find someone to share love with, someone who has love and knows it so that we can share, strengthen and demonstrate it.

Seeker: When I hear that I have to love, then I feel that I am forced to love. You also said I couldn't give love if I haven't experienced love.

Jordan: Who do you have to love? You have to love yourself by accepting yourself and by deciding what you don't like about yourself and changing it. Otherwise you will break the *law of non-force* constantly by trying to force a reaction of acceptance, recognition, understanding and pacification until you love yourself. Then, after you have changed what you don't like about yourself, you don't have to force reactions of recognition anymore. You can just be and be happy to learn from what you are being.

Compensation

I have the greatest law in the world at my disposal, and I don't even have to enact it: the *law of compensation*. We will be compensated in like measure for all the things that we ourselves do, and each of us in our own way is experiencing the *law of compensation*.

We realistically view our life and we don't deny the success we have made in the various different facets of life, and we don't limit it. We also realize that we are compensated via our understanding, our self-discipline and our awareness as to our purpose and our mission on this earth plane. There are not just the negative compensations, there are also the very positive, supportive compensations. Much of the good that comes into our life is the *law of compensation* active and expressing itself because we have begun to take more responsibility for our feelings, thoughts, words and deeds. We are activating in a more balanced way the tools that we were given upon incarnating into this physical form.

Many of the opportunities we come across on our evolutionary pathway are compensation in action to again reawaken and reestablish ourselves in our own spiritual purpose and identity and to balance those self-created, self-imposed, active limitations of identification that we have been laboring under.

In bringing balance to this *law of compensation* we have an opportunity to stop the karmic wheel as it is spinning through the individuals that through the *law of attraction* we encounter in our life. These individuals show us where we need to get back to this *law of compensation* and where we need more balance, discipline and direction.

Our children are an exact replica of our own state of mind, our emotional state and certainly of our physical attitude that was most prevalent when we begot them. We can see children mirror back to us all of our own prejudices, accepted limitations, and attitudes that we haphazardly entertained and indulged in.

The *law of compensation* works in our attitudes about our abilities and our self-worth. It works in our attitudes about our indulgence in some of our greatest fears. People in our professional areas are reacting and responding to those fears. They are reacting to our judgments of our own abilities, of our own self-worth. They are reacting to our attitudes about ourselves. They are not responding to the attitudes that we present through the persona. The persona is the face that we project for the whole world to take a look at, the face that we want people to see because we carefully painted and constructed it. But our colleagues and bosses are very much aware of our fears and our judgments and they are responding to those, even though they might not identify or categorize them. So we feel that we really haven't done a good job, but we want our boss to promote us. He does not do it, so we run to our colleagues telling them with the face that we present to the world what a victim we are because we don't get everything we think we are entitled to. Meanwhile our boss is responding to the face that we only look at occasionally, the face that says that we feel inadequate, that we haven't done a good job and that we know we could do better. So we are getting the compensation back in full force.

The *law of compensation* tells us to go back to the drawing board. What we are confronted with is showing us a malfunction between our emotional senses and our intellectual perceptions. We may evaluate it, not dissect it, not surrender to it, not indulge it, not be limited by it. We must accept it and direct it. That's the choice. Whatever we confront is showing us where we need to work on ourselves, not to work on others. We don't change our teacher; we change ourselves. We don't change our husband, our wife, society, or an illness. We change ourselves. We choose good health. So we take the medication, we have the surgery, we use the magnetic healing, we use the psychological or psychiatric treatment that exposes us to ourselves. The only struggle we've got here is the simple acceptance of who we are. Our acceptance of who we are requires direction and recognition; it requires that we do not deny what we still need and that we get it. A wise person is always aware of what he or she needs and gets it, or recognizes that he or she has it, and learns how to use it.

The *law of compensation* gives us an opportunity to take responsibility for our thoughts and our feelings and what we are experiencing, because our words and actions we govern fairly carefully.

Seeker: The *law of compensation* is actually a springboard into the more subtle areas?

Jordan: Of course. The *law of compensation* is the first law that you deal with, because you receive your compensations as women and you receive your compensations as men, but these compensations are in conjunction with the *law of cause and effect*. They exemplify behavior patterns and emotional patterns that you will follow for the entirety of your lives until you move from the *law of cause and effect* into the other laws.

Seeker: A fighter pilot is killing people while fighting for his country. How does the *law of compensation* operate?

Jordan: Either he is used as an instrument for the completion of a karma or he is activating a karma. Compensation will manifest from both actions. We must take into consideration that perhaps these people who were killed by the pilot had taken the lives of many other people in a prior life. So in this life they find it necessary to encounter war circumstances and premature disruption of the life force so that they can have an option to come to terms with the stupidity of violence, no matter under what label it is identified.

Surely, the pilot's attitude is going to have a great effect as to the degree of compensation he is going to incur. Now, is it possible for him to get the gift of grace and to be forgiven for his actions? No. His attitude determines the degree of the compensation. Does he have to labor under the compensation? Not if he applies understanding and the *law of harmlessness*.

We cannot say that his chosen profession is the cause for the injustice. The injustice is caused by man's stupidity. Can you imagine anything more stupid than entering into conflict over a religious philosophy or a piece of land that absolutely nobody owns because everybody is going to die and the land that they thought they owned isn't going to belong to them anyway? Have you ever seen a farmer's cart carrying his land and his house to the cemetery? So why would we enter into a conflict over ownership? It doesn't make sense. But we are attached to this illusion of ownership. We would be much more in conjunction with the natural laws if we saw it as custodianship, where we have custodial care for a period of time.

And that custodial care can be passed from us to someone else and be just as productive, or more so, than when it was in our hands.

Seeker: What does it mean that we do not have to labor under the *law of compensation* in action?

Jordan: It means we change our attitude about its presence and us being punished. We see ourselves as having an opportunity to learn more about ourselves and to take responsibility for those actions that we haphazardly entered into for whatever might have been our justifications. It is to know that we can redirect victim energy into creator energy, and to see how we can use the learning to be able to help other people avoid some of the same pitfalls that they may be destined to experience in degrees, but don't have to experience in the same intensity. That's how we don't labor under it. It is our determination to not let our dysfunction be a limiter in our self-image or in our ability to constructively function on this earth planet.

Cause and Effect

When we are working with the *law of cause and effect,* we can see that it is easy to evaluate the obvious, which is the effect. But we have to become much more aware of the cause that created the effect. We can continuously give an incentive, a symbol, and if they want it bad enough, they will manifest it in their own minds because they will pull out their causes, look at them and make them non-functional in their lives.

We are manipulated by and caught up in the effect. Are we wealthy? Now that is a tool. Once we look at a thing realistically we have to put faith and belief in our God being. We have to affirm constantly that we are what we haven't been in the face of all the effects that we have created by indulging in our causes. Are we loved? Do we have everything we want? As soon as we begin to prophesy it and don't allow ourselves to be distracted by our own fears, anxieties, inadequacies and even anger, we will manifest what we want and will stop blaming everyone else. We will look at everything we have created in life and we will say, "I don't want it anymore." Cause and effect says that there is an underlying cause for every existing visual effect and action in life. The only way we will get to the cause is by beginning to make the effect in our life non-effective. We can't just go home and say, "I recognize that I bought into my mother. She is controlling my life." We bought into it because we were not dealing with the cause that made us buy into it in the first place, and the cause is that we don't trust ourselves.

The truth is so simple that we want to make it complex; we want to find excuses but we don't need any. The laws are immutable. So either we work in conjunction with them or we don't. If we don't want to trace the cause by recognizing and understanding where we give our power away, then we continue to experience the effect.

If you like the results of anger, then continue to let something else have power over you. But there is an alternative—to take the power back into your hands. Are you going to get anywhere if all you ever do is look at the effect of poverty and say, "My God, it's my karma to live with this poverty." Then let it be your karma. Enjoy it. Wear it like sackcloth and ashes and be happy with it, be proud of it. You can go to the rest of the world and say, "Pity me, I am inferior, don't ask me for anything. Don't expect me to do anything; this is my karma." Then at least be proud of it and enjoy it in a balanced way because you bought it. You have to eat it, you have to sleep with it, I don't.

As for me, if I see poverty I am going to say, "Well, I see you there. What are you telling me? Where should I employ understanding, harmlessness, non-judgment, non-comparison? Which of my abilities should I use to promote my way out of the situation?" It isn't to surrender to the situation. It is to come to an understanding as to why the situation is there.

If my car stops running, it is telling me a story. If I want to get angry and limited, then I will do that. But then I might as well enjoy what I am doing. Or I can project myself into the cause and nullify the effect. Then I can get down to the compensation. Before my car stopped running, it choked and puffed

along the highway and signaled to me it needed some attention. I didn't pay attention to my car. So I've been compensated for my lack of attention. When we are dealing with the
exterior, it is easy to see the effects. But in order to get to the
cause we've got to move beyond the effect. I can't judge the
effect as a limitation. It's got to be a learning lesson, once I
produce my way through it by putting these laws into action.

Our body and emotions do the same thing, but unfortunately we keep looking for someone else to pay them the attention they need. Then when we get disappointed, the body
is our devil and our body made us do it, and we are just a
victim of circumstances. That's when we take our whip out
saying, "Father, forgive me, I didn't know what I was doing.
Father, I am punishing me. See, Father, I am obeying. Beat me
a little harder, Father. I am naughty, Father, beat me." How
long are we going to beat ourselves before we open our eyes
and decide to do something with ourselves? A journal, as simple
as it sounds will lead us to the cause. Maybe our body is not
Satan but our attitude is. Satan is actually denial, ignorance.
As soon as we employ our angelic side, which is understanding
and wisdom, then Satan and angel, the two poles, come together and create light.

In working with the *law of cause and effect* I had to come to a
realization that if I didn't like the effects that my life, my body,
my financial position, my educational limitations, and my communications were telling me, I'd better start appreciating myself. I'd better start appreciating my own beauty instead of
going around appreciating and recognizing everybody else's in
the hopes that if I did it enough, gave enough, sacrificed enough,
I would be recognized and appreciated for the beauty that I
bring into life. I learned that what I didn't like about me I
could begin to change, I could begin to understand why it was
there and how to work with it.

Seeker: If I remember the *law of cause and effect,* the minute I
         walk into an unbalanced situation—

Jordan: —it will assist you in not becoming a part of the situ-
         ation, and in being willing to take responsibility to

name and clarify the situation. When I walk into a room that is full of anger I want to find out where the strongest point of anger is. So I am going to trace it. I want to know where the anger stems from so I can do the healing process (through visualization, affirmation and other methods). I don't want to sit there like a sponge and drink it up. I want to confront it.

Psychosis and cause and effect

Seeker: Would a psychosis be the effect of a cause in a past lifetime?

Jordan: Indeed it can be. Let me give you my own personal concept of past lives and reincarnation. I've had my own experiences and I personally believe in it totally. I believe that as we descend through the atmospheric conditions, we take onto ourselves various identities and concepts that we then must work through in this lifetime. You as a teacher can only teach reincarnation and past lives as a thesis. You cannot try to influence what can only be derived experientially: the proof or the experience of reincarnation. What you will find when you start utilizing the theory of reincarnation as a means to explain away what individuals are experiencing in densified form is that you will then give them an excuse not to do anything about it. Many persons actually continue to create and recreate in their life's expression the same problems over and over again because they will not comprehend cause and effect. My answer to your question is yes.

Cancer and cause and effect

Seeker: How would a person who is diagnosed with cancer deal constructively with cause and effect?

Jordan: People who are experiencing a physical, last opportunity awareness, such as cancer, cannot continue to believe that their husbands, children, the food that they eat, the water that they drink or the land that they live on is the ultimate cause of their depletion of physical energies. It has to be brought down to the self if they are going to heal themselves. Whatever procedure they enter into in order to manifest a cure, they have to be made aware that it is the self and a change in the recognition, the direction, the understanding, and the acceptance of the self that will solidify and maintain the cure. They cannot only treat half the problem. They have to be willing to treat the whole problem, and the self is the whole problem. The parental, societal, educational, marital, and economic influences are only influences. It is the acceptance of those influences and the illusion of identity that brings about the effect. The cause simply is that they did not choose to see themselves in their true light and image. They surrendered to the influences making the illusion the prominent factor in their lives rather than getting into the actuality, which is the manifestor of life. We cannot ignore the manifestor of life on a permanent basis without creating destruction to the cell tissues. The cells have to be fed with the energy of life, the consciousness has to be fed but by a greater mind and that is universal mind.

Dissatisfactory work conditions and cause and effect

Seeker: If I am doing my work with little joy and little contentment, feeling that the compensation I am getting for it is not sufficient, how do I get to the cause?

Jordan: First by accepting the responsibility that through the *laws of attraction* and *compensation,* you've accepted a position that doesn't challenge or provide opportunity for you to exercise your extended creativity and ability, but that follows a rather secure and comfortable pathway that you feel you can master most readily. Then take a look at all of the attitudes that you find active around about you from your business associates, your co-workers, and your boss and determine whether you see yourself as superior in your understanding, intellect and endeavors to those individuals around you.

Seeker: The cause is fear of taking responsibility?

Jordan: That is part of it. The cause is unbelief in the very philosophies that you tout your great belief in. After all, wasn't it Peter who told Christ that he would defend him unto death? Peter really wanted to believe that and he certainly wanted Christ to believe it. But Christ said to him, "Before the cock crows, you will deny me three times and claim that you never knew me. But you are the rock upon which I am going to build my church." So there was Peter having to confront his unbelief. It does not always relate to a fear of taking responsibility. Sometimes it relates to a feeling of unworthiness.

Seeker: What causes us to test our belief, to enter into a situation that we feel unworthy of entering into?

Jordan: Our dissatisfaction with our surroundings. We ultimately have to take responsibility for where we are and ask what we are going to do about our dissatisfaction. We cannot avoid these laws; we cannot bend them to our own desired shape and form. They continue to work whether we recognize them or not. But eventually through dissatisfaction with our environment we must ask ourselves what if anything we are going to do about these conditions.

Illumination and cause and effect

Seeker: Is illumination the complete understanding of the cause?

Jordan: Sure. That's all it's ever been. Illumination is the understanding of the cause and the willingness to do something about it. After all, once you understand that it's your self-programming that is manifesting compensation, harmfulness, judgment, comparison, and its cause and effect, then you have no choice but to do something about it or live with it and enjoy it.

Seeker: As long as we live on the earth plane, we have not recognized to the fullest the cause of our actions?

Jordan: I will answer that question in this manner. I was talking to the Hierarchy, in another dimension of course, and I asked them why it was necessary for illuminated beings like Emil, Hilarion and St. Germain to continue to manifest themselves in physical dimensions, and if they did so why didn't we instantaneously recognize them and surrender to them and just absolutely instantaneously follow their example?

The answer I received was: When Hilarion found it necessary to take on physical density it was required that he would do this in the most degraded regions of Soho, England in order to get two parts of himself back into harmony. But with the densification he had to agree to prove himself in assuming a personality, a heritage and an identity. It was his inner light that kept him balanced as that entire karmic situation presented itself. At the right moment, amongst the thieves and the harlots of Soho, came the two parts of himself that he had come back to educate and to offer this optional choice to in order for him to move on to a higher consciousness.

So illuminated beings who choose to take on form must also agree to work with the karma of the time. In this particular case, Hilarion's incarnation was in the 19th century, under the Victorian rule with all of the expectations, etiquette and customs of the time. He had to shine brightly as an Eastern identity, dressed in his skirts, robes and turbans, while the rest of the world was in Edwardian collars with the stiff shirts. He was of course a total oddity, but he had to accept that karma and maintain his dignity.

When it is necessary for an illuminated being to incarnate in density, the being has to accept all of the karma of the country, the city, the people, the religion and the education, and the being has to remain totally neutral through the entire experience. If he had

taken on the Edwardian coats, the etiquette that ex-
emplified the stiffness and the limitation of understanding in the Victorian era, he would have taken
that karma into him and would have had to have
worked through it.

Seeker: Why don't we recognize the illuminated beings?

Jordan: Because we haven't recognized the light inside ourselves. We can't recognize illuminated beings until we
see some light inside ourselves. The first thing we are
attracted to in other human beings is not so much
the light of them, but if they are pleasing to our eye,
to our senses. Or the other side of the scale is if they
make us angry and they stir our brains into thinking.
But we don't see the light until we actually recognize
it in ourselves.

Seeker: Is anger or rage a cause or an effect?

Jordan: It's an effect.

Seeker: How can I recognize the cause behind this rage or
anger?

Jordan: It's a self-judgment of inadequacy. That's a rule of
thumb. That happens to be one of the few rules of
thumb. The concept being that you are never angry
at society, you are angry with yourself in your presentation in society. Then you trace it back to what limitation you've put on yourself.

Seeker: What can we do after we've found the cause for a
problem?

Jordan: If you find the cause of anything, you first apply acceptance to it, and then you apply discipline to it and
the *law of compensation.* You start compensating yourself by doing the things that you know you were put
on this earth plane to do. You don't allow yourself to
be limited by the effects of emotional imbalance.

Seeker: How do I find or recognize the cause?

Jordan: It can be done through meditation, through self-analy-
sis, or you can find a good psychic. You can tell him
what your obvious problem is and he can get to your
underlying imbalance. You can use psychiatry and

psychology, and they will eventually reach the same point a psychic will. That's how one finds the cause. The cause is always determined by an abuse of natural law. The cause is always a reflection of the abuse of natural law. The obvious attitudes determine the effects, but the cause is still abuse of natural law.

So you recognize a cause by not getting caught in the effect. Trace it back. Another tool to cause recognition is keeping a daily journal. When we are keeping our journal and we write down the motivation that brought about the reaction, we can trace it into our mind and understand our own limitation. Then we've got the cause and the effect.

The spiritual element and cause and effect

Seeker: Would *cause and effect* also include the spiritual element?

Jordan: Of course. I am your spiritual effect. This spiritual organization is your spiritual effect. The cause is that you have allowed yourselves, through incarnation and through the law of karma, to choose to come in to build and to create this spiritual emanation of lives, to make it prosperous and fruitful. But first you must deal with the *law of compensation* because it's been said: The more you profess poverty, the more you think poverty, the more poverty will manifest. So if the organization is dealing with poverty, isn't that compensation from every one of your mental attitudes?

Seeker: Is the ultraviolet or infrared light capable of preventing the compensation for an unbalanced thought that I've sent into the atmosphere?

Jordan: The ultraviolet can transmute it, the infrared can disintegrate it. But then it has to come back to you because you are the creator of it. It may come back transformed wearing a different face. It may come back as gaseous substance that you absorb. But you are the creator of it, so I am afraid it's going to be the garment that you are going to be wearing.

The difference between cause and effect and compensation

Seeker: Is the difference between compensation and cause and effect that compensation is what is going around and cause and effect is what is coming around?

Jordan: Compensations are the visual effects that you have in your life today. The *law of cause and effect* is what is coming down as you open the portal or the vortex for it to come down. The *law of divine order* gives you the energy and the knowledge to balance it all and make it work. The *law of like attracts like* says that everything that you experience on all dimensional levels is exactly what you are. If you are experiencing falseness on the spiritual level, it is because you are false.

As above so below

Our thoughts create our astral plane. A lot of our horror dreams or our disturbing dreams reflect our uncontrolled and undisciplined thoughts. It is in the astral dimensions where all of our embryos (thoughts) wait to be birthed forth from the womb of experience, from the womb of physical contact, and we then physically experience in densified form a reflection of our uncontrolled thoughts. That's above. As we view our world, as we create in our world, as we utilize our tools and our abilities in the world, so will we in the astral world. When we give up this physical encasement (body) and our spirit is free to leave this encasement, the first thing it has to do is move through that black place of the lower astral plane, the world that we have created. Then it goes through the tunnel into the light where it meets the Lords of the Hierarchy. There it sees on this huge screen every decision and choice we made in our life. That's when we pay our compensation because we will see how foolishly we made money our God, sex our God, public opinion our God, etc. All that we have to deal with. Then while we are waiting in that astral plane we must live in the world that we created by our thoughts until an appropriate circumstance manifests itself in kindergarten, the earth plane, and we can come back and try all over again.

The astral plane is divided into two dimensions just as man is divided into two dimensions. Man must deal with his femininity and his masculinity and with his angelic form and his satanic form. The world is created perfect, but man creates it imperfect. So we are dealing with duality. We are dealing with our receptivity in being able to view how we see and how we create the world in which we live. Here we deal with the *law of "as above so below."* When we get ourselves caught up in our intellectual identities and our personality fears, we create the reflection of those fears through our words and our actions. Our words are our children; our words we can control and direct. But our thoughts are our embryos and our embryos enter into the lower astral dimensions where they begin to take shape and form.

The lower astral realm is a composite of all of the karmic lifetimes that we are working with right here, now, today. The upper astral realm is a composite of our dharmic lifetimes. The etheric realm is the perfection of our being. So we must recognize the existence of the lower astral plane as a creation not only of our past lifetimes but also of this present existence. Our past life imbalances have been strengthened by our words, actions and thoughts in this lifetime, and they gain more strength from like thoughts and like actions. Birds of a feather flock together; water seeks its own level. We can see the truth of that in our mates, in our occupations, in how we are expressing ourselves, and in how we create the lower astral dimensions. So while we indulge in all of our distractions and confusions, we only are attracting those distractions and those confusions as actual physical experiences.

We know what is above must be below and what is below must be above. So all of our thoughts exist out there in those unseen dimensions and also in this very dense dimension, in this very seen atmosphere that we've created for ourselves. That means we have the opportunity to create a vortex that allows us to be able to move through this personal karmic dimension and create this channel of a wonderful awareness of the living avatar of ourselves.

We can experience many energy patterns existing within

the atmosphere, but they don't have life until we give it to them. That's how it is possible to have spirit exteriorly and spirit interiorly. It is in conjunction with the *law of "as above so below."* Whatever we recognize and give energy to is life. Otherwise it's just existence, it's just there. Our spirit forces literally can have no effect on us until we give them life, until one part of our mind desires the assistance and the upliftment to free ourselves from our mundane situations.

As we think of the *law of "as above so below,"* we must remember that what we do today, right now, we are doing in the astral world and only during the sleep state, when the mind is at an ebb, do we have an opportunity to sometimes experience what we have created out here in the astral world. We've got to clean that out; nobody else is going to come and clean it out for us. Meditation prepares us for that job. Every one of our thoughts, our feelings and our actions, though they may not represent themselves immediately in the physical world, represent themselves immediately in the astral world, the lower astral world.

The *law of "as above so below"* tells us why symbols, parables and prose are so very, very important in our lives because life in itself, as we know it in the physical dimension, is a symbol. A symbol is an existing energy that denotes an action taking place in the atmosphere; in the dense atmosphere of physical life, in the less dense atmosphere of lower astral manifestation and in the etheric dimensions. It is an illusion of an accepted concept, an accepted reality, but beneath that reality there is an existing actuality. In order for us to understand the actuality we must understand the reality and we must know how and why the reality is manifested.

Hell and the law of "as above so below"

According to the assimilation of energies from the lower astral plane and according to the *law of "as above so below"* we humans are assimilations of atom structure, which is just another description of energy, infused and limited by a karmic/dharmic personality. We project a living embryo, which is shapeless and formless but nonetheless living energy, into that lower astral plane.

There is where our hell is, because from the lower astral

plane descends, via our physical, geographical, continental, societal and personal karmas, that which we must learn to balance and work with as we work through the passage of time—from birth to the time of demise. That's where you will find your loved ones if they believe that heaven is a state where there is rocking chairs, little white cottages and things of that nature. That is exactly what they will get because that is what they have created.

If they have created totally from their personality ego and they only see themselves in their personality ego assimilation of personality, when they give up this physical density and the spirit is released from the body it does not skip from point A to point Z. It does not pass by all of the other places that it has created. It goes right there to the lower astral.

Follow-up dialogue

Seeker: So after we make the transition we have to go through the hell of all the out of balance thoughts that we have created?

Jordan: Of course. In the "Life and Teaching of the Masters of the Far East" they describe in detail a huge screen where you see all of your unbalanced actions, thoughts, emanations and choices manifested right there in front of you. And you have to work them out. If you accept the concept of reincarnation, then you realize we are here to work out what afflicts us.

Seeker: When we judge someone and we die, we indeed will experience that judgment in the astral plane?

Jordan: Absolutely.

Seeker: How is it different from experiencing judgment on the earth plane? Is it more intense?

Jordan: Is it more intense? Down here we have the cushioning of our personalities, and that always represents a great shock absorber for us. We always have freedom of choice, we can either discipline our personalities or we can indulge them. We can always walk out of our marriages, walk away from our teachers and continue to create life as a reflection of our own imbalance. Or we can decide to stick it out and discipline ourselves and perhaps know that our teachers are really teaching us for our own good. But divorce in this society has become so prevalent and everybody is afraid to make a commitment. It is much easier not to have any paper that reminds you that you've got any commitment other than your own particular desire. It is much easier in the physical. In the lower astral plane you don't have any personality because that goes with your body; you just see the reflection of it, you are just energy.

Mediumship and the law of "as above so below"

Seeker: Do the physical trumpets need to be present in order for the etheric trumpets to manifest in the séance room?

Jordan: Does a physical body need to be present for the materialization to manifest itself in a room?

Seeker: Yes.

Jordan: You've got your answer. "As above so below." Why do we have all the icons? They are a physical manifestation of an etheric or an astral concept. They are the physical interpretation of an existing life force.

Seeker: Because of "as above so below" do our spirit guides have the same personality that we interpret?

Jordan: They don't have a personality, and you haven't become their personality because you are still dealing with your interpretation.

Seeker: When we go to sleep we give ourselves to our spirit forces. Do we program that we want to do healing while in the sleep state, or do we leave that up to spirit?

Jordan: Both. We have to work through the lower astral plane, which contains our creations. Remember the *laws of attraction* and *"as above so below."* When we become a working practitioner of our spiritual arts, whether that's in music, healing, counseling, teaching or whatever, we work on many dimensional realms. In our sleep state we must first move through the lower astral level. That's where our nightmares, confusions, and feelings of anxiety come from. Because of this *law of attraction,* because we are a light, a flame inside our being—like the moths coming to the flame— the "moths" are going to be attracted not only to our light but to the similar thought processes we are going to have to work with. That's what we call soul saving.

When we get into the upper astral realm we begin to recognize the divine order of things, and that's where we begin to do our greatest work. As a light in our altered state of sleep we are actually generating an energy power into the atmosphere. Oftentimes this is expressed in the physical dimension by prayer groups that get together in harmony and affirm the divine order of things. They are looking at the physical results, but they are actually affirming the divine order of things. They pray for the universe, the sick, their church, financial solvency, loved ones, etc. We can do much more with thoughts than we can with spoken words. So, yes, with the *law of attraction* your hardest job is to get beyond that lower astral plane.

At the end of the day just before you fall asleep, simply affirm in your mind that you are turning yourself over to universal mind, to your teachers and guides and to the purpose of fulfillment. Say these words: "Father God, all things prophesied and predicted this day, let them be done in accordance with your will and not mine." That absolutely nullifies karma. Let me explain that to you. Each of us makes snap judgments from our states of consciousness and awareness. It is part of life. But as we become more illuminated and more enlightened, we have to take responsibility and recognize that it is the divine consciousness of ourselves and the divine consciousness of humanity that is actually bringing the manifestation into solidification. That's how I have been able to avoid karma with all of the situations and circumstances that I have had to work with in my career as a teacher. That's the *law of attraction*. The minute I clear myself of that karma, I don't have to play in the lower astral realms. I can zoom right up to the higher astral realm, the etheric realm and the cosmic realm because I am not limited by my own creations.

Attraction

It is the *law of attraction* that has caused people to put their energy 100 percent into assimilating a fortune, or a great publicly recognized career in show business, politics, religion or any of the other expressions. But they had to see some example that they wanted to be just like before they could attract it.

Through the *law of attraction* we attract to us on social, geographical, continental, universal, personal, family and educational levels everybody that we are karmically, in some way, shape and form, indebted to or dharmically associated with. It is up to us to know whether it is a karmic or dharmic association.

The *law of attraction* attracts individuals who are the embodiment of the many facets of our own being, and we can view these facets in physical expression. We may elect out of our own fears or out of our own self-imposed limitations to ignore what we are seeing, but that's a fool's paradise. Because at some point we will experience it in our physical expression, in life. We know that we actually communicate with our actions, our words and our thoughts. We also know that thoughts are things, that they are actually living energies that precede our verbal expression and our physical action. They are out there and through the *law of attraction* bring into manifestation learning lessons for us so that we can work through them.

We live in a society that we have created. It is a reflection and an expression of our own emotional fears, anxieties, judgments, encapsulations, and doubts. As a result we experience it physically, in the physical dimension. It has been said that if we fear a consequence, we will actually experience it. If we fear being robbed, we will actually experience being robbed; if we fear being denied or rejected, we will actually be denied and rejected because the *law of attraction* will bring it to us.

We must face our horrors, then we will understand ourselves and we will be able to understand others. For example, we must understand ourselves and our use of money, power and communication before we can go into a struggling company and discover accurately where its executives, employees and bosses are misusing power, money, communication to destructively influence and affect humanity.

We must understand ourselves, then we will see the cause of a mental breakdown much more clearly. As we understand ourselves we will see why sometimes psychiatry isn't working properly and chemicals are used rather than common sense communication. If you go into a mental institution, you will find brilliant people struggling under sedation because the practitioners are not educated enough to cope with the dysfunctions that the patients are demonstrating. So it is easier to keep them quiet, pacified. But how often do we sedate and pacify ourselves through our abundant consumption of so many distractions and excuses, explanations and justifications that we give to ourselves?

Why do we have terrorism? Think how we terrorize one body with the other; how we terrorize our mental body with our spiritual body, think of how we impatiently try to break our mental body away from its sense of security. We terrorize our mental security with our spiritual desire for supremacy. We terrorize our physical body with all our paranoid emotions, and our emotions are just sure that the whole world is ready to jump on us and abuse us. All those sensations are sent to our physical body, and it has to respond to all this terroristic treatment. And as for thievery, think about how we cheat ourselves and our government(s).

We must view, accept and understand ourselves as an individual universe creating and functioning amongst and within a collective universe. In order for us to affect the collective universe in a balanced, constructive, supportive way we must balance our individual universe. This requires us going inside. Never give the power exteriorly. I take great offense with anybody who encourages anyone to seek the answers to mastery exteriorly, for any reason, because the answers will only be found inside yourself. It's like creating a road map that allows you to go from Saturn to Venus without distraction, limitation and obstacles. Always remember that everything is theoretical in your consciousness until it's been experienced, and you will only experience it by activating it first within and then expressing it without. It would be wonderful if we could find all of the answers in the effects that we are encountering, in the effects of the active energy that is out there having its minute receptive influence on that universe, first interior and then exterior. It would be lovely if we could discover all the answers exteriorly and tap into that ever present energy pattern that many dreamers and geniuses see. But some of them fail in their intent because they lose their direction by expecting it all in the exterior. The only road map for successful use of what is exterior is through discovering first of all its presence interiorly and opening those portals so that we can magnetically attract it, manifest it, densify it, and use it. But first we must find it inside. And we must become it.

In working with the *law of attraction* we must recognize that many times in our astral journeys, especially during the sleep state, we are encountering those unrecognized thoughts and feelings that we have unknowingly released into the astral dimension. While we are there we are dealing with some things in symbols, and as we record them and bring them back, we have then the opportunity to start projecting compensating energies into that astral dimension so that they do not gain strength, power and dimension and manifest as an existing experience.

For example, individuals that are unconsciously projecting a fear of being cheated will find that they will go through life constantly experiencing being cheated until they recognize that this is a thought that they are continuously projecting. It becomes, because of the *law of attraction,* dense, dimensional and a happening. Individuals who are afraid of being disapproved of are constantly projecting that fear of disapproval, and as a result, the *law of like attracts like* magnetically pulls all of those disapproving fears into the astral plane, and then it becomes a happening. Individuals who are mistrusting and transfer their mistrust onto their mates, project that mistrust until, because of the *law of like attracts like,* it becomes a dimensional factor, an influence, and all of a sudden they find that their mates are cheating on them. Then they've got to live with it, work with it.

In order to get love we have to be love. In order to get honesty we have to be honest; not with society, with ourselves. When we're being honest with ourselves, we're being honest with society. Love, honesty is the symbol of what we are. We are talking about the symbols of life, and we are clarifying them in words because words and actions are what we buy into. Success is the symbol of being success. In order to experience the symbol of happiness, we must be happy inside ourselves. We cannot be unloving and attract love. We can't be feminine and expect to attract masculinity, because we are only going to attract femininity. We cannot be totally materialistic and expect to attract spiritual vibrations. We must vacillate between the two poles inside of ourselves. We must have inner peace in order to attract the exterior symbols of peace. If we are dealing with a symbolic exterior world that reflects our interior world, then we can look at all of the symbols, the universal symbols that are around us, and recognize that interiorly we are in a disharmonious balance with the universe.

Our emotional body, intellectual body, spiritual body and physical body will attract a like dimensional energy. It is up to us to increase that dimensional energy.

Suppose in the physical realm you have done the exercises to make yourself physically attractive. So you emanate an energy that says, "I am attractive. I am desirable. I am confident." Yet, intellectually you say, "I don't know enough. I am not in control enough. I don't have enough." Then emotionally you say, "I am an absolute total disaster." Now, on the physical plane, you will get many people wanting your body, but no one wanting your brain and absolutely no one wanting to really merge with you emotionally, unless they are of a like nature, which means they are just as much emotionally out of balance as you are. Knowing yourself tells you exactly what it is you have attracted.

In the *law of like attracts like,* you can't simply say, "I am going to control my mind." You must control your emotions, your physical actions, and you must understand them. It is not enough to just control them. Then you'd become nothing more than a robot, and God didn't intend us to be robots. Every statement that comes out of our mouth, we live with. That's why it is so important for us to watch our statements. Thoughts are our embryos; words are our children. The words we say we can never take back, for they live as children in the hearts of those who experience them.

Manifestation and the law of attraction

Seeker: When we attract a like energy, does that always manifest in another person?

Jordan: It can come in the form of another person, but remember that a person is nothing more than densified energy. When you begin to really train your mind to accept the concept that a person is densified energy expressing through karmic and dharmic influences, it's going to help you to be much more receptive to the situations all around about you. Yes, you coagulate them and you give them life as Jane Doe, or as mother, father, brother, sister, boss, employee and so forth, but that's just a densified energy that is assimilated to fulfill particular purposes. When you recognize that you can understand the personality influences that are karmic/dharmic, then it can help you to perceive what energy to begin to project, to emulate from inside of yourself to counteract what energy patterns you encounter.

We have the right at all times to work with the laws of transmutation and to not be hindered or limited in our evolutionary processes by those out of balance forms of energy patterns that we encounter when we recognize the *law of attraction,* when we recognize the rising of kundalini and we are dedicated and disciplined to go through the necessary processes to bring about the evolution that would attract that like energy from the atmospheric conditions.

So, yes, like energy can come in the form of a physical being, but it doesn't have to. It could take on the form of a spirit guide, of a universal teaching energy, of an atmospheric condition, of a geographical location, of a house, of music, of color, of an animal. It could take on any form. It can be whatever stimuli that will help you move through the blockade that is self-induced and self-created.

Seeker: What is the difference between the *law of like attracts like* and the *law of compensation?*

Jordan: The *law of like attracts like* deals with the emotional body, and the *law of compensation* deals with the intellectual mind and the active action. Many of you have been compensated, because of your disciplines, with certain results but the results are not as satisfactory as they could be if you would apply the *law of attraction*. You all make yourselves in the forms that make you desirable to other people, and then you wonder why your desirability is not long lasting. It's because of the *law of attraction*. You are attracting exactly what you are programming for yourselves. It's easy to starve yourself and lose weight, it's easy to build a physical countenance to attract beautiful people to you, but it's very hard to maintain it. And, all the time you lose people left and right, that shows you that you are unbalanced in your emotional bodies.

The *law of compensation* is what you do and what you say. The *law of like attracts like* is what you feel and think. From the *law of compensation* you can tell what you ultimately, eventually feel and think. In order to conquer the *laws of like attracts like* and *compensation* and to stand as a third person between your angelic self and your satanic self, you must first know yourself. When you are jealous, ask what you haven't been doing that you should have done, for whatever intellectual reason. Be willing to pay the price that your higher self says you are going to pay. Then change yourself. When spirit indicates to you what you should be doing, do it. Don't say, "I'll do it tomorrow," because tomorrow may never come. That's how you get to know yourself. You don't justify. When you know you should be somewhere, be there. When you know you should be doing something, do it. All laws eventually will come into physical manifestation.

Relationships—the law of attraction in action

Seeker: I have seven children. They all show me the *law of attraction* in action?

Jordan: Yes, you have seven composites of your emotional, mental attitudes while you and your husband were what you would call making love. So I am quite sure you have beautiful examples right in front of you of both your balanced and your unbalanced qualities and understandings as your children become such wonderful mirrors for you.

Seeker: If we live alone for a while after a separation, how can we use that time wisely so that we don't attract, according to the *law of attraction,* the same problematic situation in the next relationship?

Jordan: By doing some self-talk and by asking each of your bodies singularly what it expected to get and didn't, what it truly wanted to create and couldn't—for whatever the justification may have been. Ask yourself what physical traits were most disruptive in the consciousness of the individual and what physical traits you would have liked him or her to have had. For example, you might not have liked the fact that your chosen companion came to bed with dirty feet. You may not have liked that your companion read a newspaper at the table instead of talking to you.

Do a whole evaluation and ask yourself what it is that you want. That helps you to get more in touch with what is important to you and it prepares you to be able to do trade-off once you are attracting your next companion. You start giving it to yourself, and in the process you attract the companion who is also giving to himself what is important to him. Then you have so much more to share, to express with each other. So both of you are in a self-discovery process. You are working together because you have recognized what is important. But you can't do that while you are finding fault, while you are justifying or while you are taking the responsibility entirely on yourself.

Being unconscious of a tendency and the law of attraction

Seeker: Sometimes I am unconscious of what I am doing. Does the *law of attraction* still work the same way?

Jordan: We want to believe that we are unconscious of many things that we do, but we can't afford to be unconscious. We must be conscious of every action, every thought, every word that leaves our mouths. We must elect in which direction we are going to direct our energies because where we direct our energies brings about experiences in physical dimension according to the *laws of attraction* and *compensation* that we do not want to live with. We get what we ask for, and we ask for things in various levels. So it is important for us to recognize and know ourselves. Once we know ourselves, we stand a better chance of being able to direct our energy flow so that we can leave the limiting circumstances we find ourselves in and experience the bounty that is there because God created a perfect world. It's only man's comprehension of it that makes it imperfect.

We have tools such as colorology, philosophy, religion, graphoanalysis, numerology, astrology, etc., in order to determine what we are not always conscious of or what we refuse to be conscious of. We do dream interpretation and dream analysis and we keep journals so that we can reach into those areas where our consciousness has us blocked and determine what we are really asking for. Because we always get out of life what we really ask for.

Divine Order

When we activate mentally, emotionally and physically this *law of divine order* it stops us from feeling, seeing and creating ourselves as a victim. Many of us go through life being an emotional victim, believing that we are constantly being punished or harassed from some factor of society because we don't see things as being in divine order and as opportunities for learning. We see things as absolutely desperate and we see ourselves as being the victim of this desperation. Once we see ourselves as the victim of the circumstances that we are creating in life, then unfortunately, we are totally in need of someone else doing it for us. Because we give our power away, we are dependent on the good graces and the good wishes of someone else. Then we are not required to do anything about these conditions and circumstances affecting us.

We must see God in action in politics. But sometimes we forget that no matter how we interpret a thing, how we feel a thing, or an action, it is in divine order. We've got to see through all of our distorted interpretations and reactions to discover divine order functioning.

God has a purpose for everything under the sun, just as he has a purpose for everything behind the sun. We must learn to see divine order functioning in all of the situations and circumstances that we have been responsible for creating and put God in action with them.

Man's law is formulated so that we can in some respect express a likeness and unity. We are individual and unique, and in that uniqueness we each accept a portion of the divine concept identity. Man's law says that we must look beautiful according to man's concept of beauty, but natural law says that everything is in divine order. Man's law causes us to judge ourselves: we aren't living up to our standards and expectations. Divine order says, "You are in order as long as you are listening to me." Natural law says we are already beautiful; man's law says we have to be beautiful according to its concept.

The tree grows without assistance from man. The grass grows, the flowers bloom, the water flows and the seasons change. They don't need any help from man. Man doesn't have to do a thing for the seasons to change. Without man there will be spring, summer, autumn and winter. The bird will fly, the rose will bloom. The wild cherries, the apples, the pears will also blossom and bloom without man. If man just leaves them alone, they will take care of themselves.

Divine order is to see that everything has a purpose and that nothing happens by chance.

As I stand right now before you I am in divine order according to God intelligence. I am perfect as he made me, for everything about me is going to bring me information that I am going to employ in my future creations. I can begin clearing the past away by saying: As I am right now, fat, old, young, ugly, well, unwell, I am perfectly in divine order because this is how I have created me, how I have viewed me. This is my information that is going to help me to make some decisions in my life about what I want to be, emulate and create.

In working with the *law of divine order* we don't see things as a tragedy, we see things as information. I see all actions as being a part of divine order. I can recognize and understand the conditions that individuals bring to me, but if I only gave them sympathy, pity and empathy, I would never get to working with the soul that says that they are better than they think they are. It takes a split second to say everything is right in God's world or in divine order. We apply the *law of divine order* by leaving people exactly where they want to be, knowing that it is okay for them.

That will make it much easier to activate that Christ principle, and the Christ principle can be identified with the *law of divine order* because, regardless of how we interpret the circumstances and the situations that we see activated in our society, families and professions, things are in divine order if we detach from the temporality of the existence, learn from it and see the balance that is beneath the experience.

When we keep identifying a person as suffering from cancer

we are actually projecting the energy patterns that continue to activate cancer as opposed to wellness, because we are seeing cancer as a destructive force. I see it as an opportunity. I see all identified illnesses, all situations as opportunity for greater self-discovery.

The Christ consciousness and divine order

Seeker: Would you give us some assistance to activate the Christ consciousness within us? I am working with an affirmation, saying, "I am one with the Christ con-sciousness." I am trying to express it with my fellow men and in my work. But it is very difficult.

Jordan: Perhaps it is difficult because you are still in some degree entering into sympathy, empathy and pity, all of which make you superior. From a superior stand-point, you are going to separate yourself from that active principle inside of yourself.

Activate this *law of divine order* through affirmation when you confront individuals before you activate separation from your Christ principle inside, from the Christ being. Look at that blemish of that character-istic and see it in divine order as a learning opportu-nity for the individuals. Don't see yourself as being affected by it, but ask yourself what's your purpose in being there.

The Desiderata, as an affirmation, reminds us to be non-attached and retain our center in our Christed prin-ciple. It's as simple as that. The affirmation "I am in God and God is in me, we are in oneness" is, again, an affirmative power that detaches us from physical per-sonality identity as the doctor, as the human being. Whether we have chosen a male body or a female body as our tool, those are important affirmations and yes, indoctrinations. For example, the minute we attach to poverty we own it. I see poverty as an opportunity and I affirm and support wealth. I affirm equality, not inferiority and superiority. I refuse to see dys-function as anything other than an opportunity.

Seeker: If you know that someone who is planning to come to your class is going to create a disturbance in the class, would you actually ask that person not to come?

Jordan: I would not ask that person not to come. I tell Tall Pine (my guiding force) to make it impossible for the individual to come. I always let my spirit forces do the work for me. I simply tell Tall Pine that he is going to create a disturbance. Then Spirit's good judgment will create situations that will make it impossible for him to come. If he is already in the class, he will walk out. And, it's not interfering with the *law of divine order* when I let Spirit do it. It is interfering in divine order if I say, "Get the hell out of my class, you are no good." A student has just as much responsibility as the teacher does if the student is really sincere in his desire to evolve.

Seeker: A family member is ill. The rest of the family sees her as ill. I see her as perfect. But I don't want to fight the rest of the family so what is my responsibility?

Jordan: To treat her as a human being. Beyond that you have no control. Some of the people will learn without you saying a word. I would rather see a sermon any day than hear one. Be a sermon. If you are, then you stop criticizing and condemning the people that aren't. That's where divine order comes in. If everything is in divine order, we do not beat doors down to try to convince people that what we are doing is right. That is only our need to prove to ourselves that what we are doing is right.

In order to do transmutation we must entertain the idea that everything is energy vacillating in various different frequencies. Thought is energy, feeling is energy, word is energy, objects are energy vacillating in various different frequencies. So we must discover that behind each presentation of molecular structure there is an existing energy pattern that is balanced. We do that by identifying with the law that all things are in divine order, that all things that can be labeled and identified have a productive purpose. That means there is no wrong, there is no right, there is just learning. So we must be prepared to look at the forms that every object takes to determine the indwelling learning or balanced use of it. We rarely, if ever, get attached to a form. We practice non-attachment. Every form must serve a purpose and bring information, whether it's cancer, tuberculosis, money, gems, metal, medicine, etc.

Giving our all and the law of divine order

Seeker: What shall we do if we catch ourselves with negative thoughts that we haven't given our all?

Jordan: The best thing to do is to understand what you expected to be fulfilled. Every time I begin to evaluate myself as a teacher, I do so only after I have decided that I have given my all to the situation, to my teaching profession. If each day I give my all to anything and everything, then I can trust the *law of divine order.* I can know that if I have done what I expected of myself, I will reap the harvest because I generate a sense of well-being.

Apply that in a business sense. If I get up in the morning and I expect to be in the office at x-hour, to have my desk in order and to have the calendar worked out for the day so that I am not overstressed or indulgent, then I have met my expectations. At my first client's call, I feel good about myself. I feel so good about what I am doing that I automatically send out good thoughts to my client and they come back. The *law of compensation* and the *law of divine order* work. But if I am resenting the fact that I am in the office, if I am resenting the interference of family, business partners or a boss, because I really don't want to work, then I have made myself a failure and absolutely everything goes wrong. If I want to grow spiritually, I arise in the morning and following the *laws of compensation* and *divine order,* I say, "Today is God's day." Then

I look at what God has given me to do during the day.

Seeker: What can we do when we haven't given our all?

Jordan: Start giving your all. That's a simple answer. But you would like to see instant results, instant gratification, and you are not willing to wait, to clear up your muck and mire. So you never give your all. You give it for two days, and then you take it back because you haven't gotten instant gratification.

You will never get anything until you have given your all to it. You give your all to it, and I guarantee you, you'll come out successfully.

"It Matters Not"

We can really only apply the *law of "it matters not"* when we have a tremendously good concept of our own self. Otherwise we are just indulging ourselves, but fooling ourselves into thinking that we apply "it matters not." In reality, until we know and accept ourselves, this law does not apply to us. Because from an unconscious and subconscious realm it does matter and we respond as if it matters. We allow ourselves to get affected by the opinions, the encapsulations and the limitations that others place upon us because we projected it outwardly. It is only when we know ourselves, accept ourselves and are working with ourselves that we can, from a subconscious and unconscious realm, apply the *law of "it matters not."* Some of us might indulge in our adherence to man's laws instead of natural laws and we are going to say, "It doesn't matter." But it does matter because only when we recognize and accept who we are, can we apply the *law of "it matters not."*

When we start applying the *law of "it matters not"* we respond, react and create from our highest degree of intelligence. We do not look to someone else for verification of what we have seen. This law is very important because all through our life we are going to have to understand it, apply it and utilize it. We want to apply it when we work with humanity, because from each experience we get a greater understanding of our own self, and from that understanding we derive the opportunity to grow.

Let's say a lady wants to advance her mediumship and ministerial ability. She has fought through all of man's laws that say it's impossible. But, she has never been able to lose that awareness of her responsibility as a medium and a minister. So she fights with all of man's laws and her concept of them until she begins to apply the *law of "it matters not."* She decides it does not matter what her husband thinks or what anyone else thinks. What matters is that she performs her duties, her self-imposed obligations, and if she performs them, she is in conjunction with the *law of "it matters not."*

A man feels a desire to move into a position, and of course, to me a position is always an expression of all the qualities within ourselves. His first encounter is going to be his fellow man or man's laws. As he comes to an understanding of his purpose, he will build the bridge to natural laws. He will see man's expectations and know God's recognition. He will be the middle pillar that projects God's recognition in an acceptable way. He can only project that recognition by following the *law of "it matters not."*

It is easy to apply the *law of "it matters not"* once we understand why we are doing a thing. That means that we are prepared to deal with and encounter whatever imbalance or balance comes our way. We are willing to look at it, accept it, and work with it.

"It matters not" is a real attitude. It matters not what another man thinks of us because he is only showing himself what he thinks of himself. So we don't have to go through life struggling for humanity's good opinion. We can go through life recognizing humanity's opinion. It doesn't matter if today a man thinks me a fool, for tomorrow he might think me a genius, and if he thinks that I am a genius today, tomorrow he may think I am a fool. So it does not matter, does it? What matters is what we think of ourselves. Do you realize how many people sell their soul because it matters to them what people are going to say about them, what the family is going to think about them, what the woman or man sitting next to them is going to think about them? Think of all the denial that we enter into because we are not in conjunction with this *law of "it matters not.*" What should matter is what you think about yourself, what you know about yourself.

So we are talking about attitudes. All of our attitudes are constantly affecting our chakras. We produce the blockade and limit the flow of the fires of kundalini so that we are not totally aware of our unity with everything—the earth, the atmosphere, the plant life, the animal kingdom, the mineral kingdom. This prohibits our utilization of the energy forces for the alchemist's process of transmutation.

How can you expect to evoke the laws or the affirmations of St. Germain for transmutation, for alchemy, when you are still attached to the form? You have to see beyond the form into the reality in order to truly use alchemy. I don't care how much of the hermetic science you expose yourself to, you are never going to be able to transmute matter into its original form until you can see its original form. When you are still attached to the form you will not be able to know what the matter symbolically represents and what purpose it serves. It's the whole secret of knowing the basic chemicals that make up the whole process of alchemy, whether it's hermetic or any of the other ancient arts and practices. So you'd better practice "it matters not." The form is of very little importance. It is how the form is used that is important.

Seeker: When I work with my patients and start worrying what they might think about me, I apply the *law of "it matters not."* Can I do that, or should I do something else?

Jordan: You should be concerned about what you are thinking about yourself while you are doing your work. I am not so much concerned about what you are going to think about me as I am concerned about what I am going to think about myself. I am always very concerned about what I am going to channel, what I am going to present, and that I will do my utmost to present only the best. Once I recognize that I am dealing with my own anxieties and fears, then I can nullify the actions of those persons that would be in association with me by simply nullifying my own. We are a sending and a receiving set, and we can't fool the world. In fact, we really don't fool anybody because all of our anxieties and fears are projected outwardly. Individuals we come into contact with are receptive to the very emanation of energies that we are projecting. That's where the *law of "it matters not"* comes into action. If I evaluate that I am one of the finest teachers and phenomena mediums in the world today, and I know that I've put forth the energy to make myself that way, then I can conquer my personality ego concerns as to what you may think about me. As long as I know that I have prepared the way to be the best of what I am at that moment in time, then I can apply the *law of "it matters not,"* because I know that my emanation is going to be balanced and not one that would attract negative or unbalanced reactions. Then I can say "it matters not," because by saying that it puts a light of protective energy around me, as I've already accepted and already know myself. I know the product I am selling is the best. I know that my presentation of the product I am selling is the best at that level and that degree. As a result, I will be less affected by my absorption of your thoughts, actions and words. I am not emanating a need for approval from outside sources because I am approving of myself.

The *law of "it matters not"* comes to us first and it must "matter not" what state of consciousness we are in because it can only eventually bring evolution.

Harmony

The *law of harmony* is that conjunctional law that brings about a unity between the elements: earth, fire, water and air. It takes us out of our assimilated personality identity and puts us in a flexible vibratory rate where we can harmonize with the vibration of the water, the atmosphere, the earth and all things therein. It brings us flexibility so that we can derive the messages, the communication, the insight that will help us to avoid the problematic situations that an overextension of pressure on the earth's surface within the plant kingdom, the animal kingdom and the atmosphere would manifest. It's more or less entering into an altered state of harmony with our own inner being, our own chemical makeup, and listening. It's the realization that absolutely everything responds to love, tenderness and appreciation. Instead of seeing division and separation we should see unification with understanding and a clear-sighted recognition of the purposes that all things serve. We should see how we will utilize that purpose if we recognize the value of that purpose and are flowing along with that purpose. It's being in harmony with ourselves. That's how we begin it. To be in harmony with ourselves, we must love ourselves, appreciate ourselves, indeed, be tender to ourselves and direct ourselves. We do not have to like all of our creations, but we must love them. When we are disharmonious with ourselves, then compensation sets in and we are disharmonious with everybody else. Then we find a static in the atmosphere that says: stop, look, listen and learn.

We are out of harmony with the world when we are resistant to our creations. First we have to evaluate realistically the outer conditions. They are not there as a punishment. We are not being punished, but punish ourselves. The conditions are there to show us that we are out of harmony with ourselves. We are not harmonious with our feeling, which requires our solar plexus. We are not harmonious with our love, which requires our heart chakra. We are not harmonious with our understanding, which requires our third eye chakra. We are holding on to our own self-denials, resistance and lack of recognition. I am what I am and what I am bears no excuses, requires no explanation.

It is so important to be harmonious in this time. Our world is totally out of harmony through the negative energies of our own denials and resistances that we've put into the atmosphere. We are burning away our protective ozone layers. We are absolutely depleting our soil protection measures. And we are in overabundance effecting disorders, malfunctions in our immune system, which are causing us to be the recipient and the expression of emotional disorder, physical disorder, mental incapability. If we don't do something now to become more harmonious, we can expect to be the most deprived nation, the most deprived universe. It begins now with us becoming harmonious with ourselves. Our harmony can't depend on our family or anyone else. It has to depend on us alone. We can only evaluate our utilization of our life-force energy and see where we are bound in our own self-punishment and destruction. We can be in conjunction with the *law of harmony* by applying the *law of non-judgment,* by being aware intuitively and inspirationally, and by looking realistically at the situations that we have created. We must stop seeing them as a punishment, as a monument to our lack of balanced utilization of our life-force energy. We are so resistant and denying because we don't want to see our outer manifestations as our creations.

I don't create other people's worlds. But if I respond to them inharmoniously, and I don't apply a balanced expression of love in people's creation of their world, and I intensify their imbalance through pity, sympathy and empathy, then I have accepted their actions into my world. Our own harmony has to be established. Then and only then will each of us see clearly how to be the healer, the teacher and the way shower.

Harmlessness

Here is how we break the *law of harmlessness:* We want to express our higher consciousness. We want to be free from limitations. We want to experience the goodness of life. What keeps us from it is our comparison, judgment, denial and omission. Also, we don't recognize the value of thoughts; we won't see the importance of controlling them. We'll control our words so we don't get a reaction of disharmony. But we won't control our thoughts so we can control our destinies. Our destinies are in our hand. We'll make every excuse to not put into practice the *law of harmlessness,* and we'll make everybody else responsible for our choices.

Man's law says: You shall not kill. Metaphysicians know that we can kill as much with our thoughts, words, and judgments as we can kill with a gun, a knife, a blunt instrument, a poison, a rope, etc. Many of us in our physical practices would never kill another individual. We are too disciplined, too evolved for that. But with our words we would judge, encapsulate, gossip. We would kill someone in degrees and inches with our mouth, and we would have a thousand and one excuses as to why we are doing it. The most destructive killing is what we do with our thoughts when they are uncontrolled. As a result we have broken this *law of harmlessness.*

The *law of harmlessness* and nature

Nature will heal itself when we stop abusing it, when we learn to work in conjunction with nature, to see ourselves as a part of nature and to derive the necessary insights that nature offers us into our own characteristic actions. We would certainly be much further along in our expression of our evolution. As we become harmless and practice harmlessness we can go into nature and be the healers we were meant to be. We can project those compensating energies to everything that expresses life, and we can learn to live in harmony.

Early in my career I had a friend who liked to cook. One day she found that ants had invaded her kitchen cabinets, and to a cook that is quite a disaster. These creatures were everywhere. To make things worse she expected guests for dinner. So her first reaction was anger. Then, because we were involved in this metaphysical understanding, she decided to talk to the ants. The ants were communicating that they were hungry and she had an abundance. So she said to the ants: "If I give you food outside, will you stay outside and not invade my cabinets? If you invade my cabinets again, I am going to send you to the other side of life." Apparently the answer she got back was yes. So periodically during the week, she checked their food supply outside, which was made up of sugar and flour, and she never had ant problems again. She was perfectly harmless to herself in telling them that if they came into the house again she would send them to ant heaven, but that she would meet their request and give them food outside. That was a great demonstration of the *law of harmlessness* and where it actually begins.

Sometimes to be harmless has been interpreted to mean to be harmless to the animal kingdom and not to eat meat because it is a life force that pollutes the human organ, cell, muscular, and blood systems. There are whole philosophies built on the concept of harmlessness to the animal kingdom, saying that we practice an act of violence if we kill a fly (even though we know that flies carry all of the germs and destructive elements from the garbage and all of the other elements that they feed on in nature).

We have taken the rudimentary concept of harmlessness, but have forgotten that we are one of God's creatures, too. So we have to work with this law on ourselves and cease to be destructive to ourselves. Oftentimes, as we are attempting to avoid being seen as an egotist, we break this *law of harmlessness.* As a result, we lessen our own value in our communications to others when we give a low opinion of our self, our intelligence, our capabilities, our own physical self.

Few of you would say, "I am the best teacher in the world." You just would not do that because someone would possibly think you were an egotist. You would not say that you are the best healer, the best female, the best male person in the world. You would not say that you are infinitely rich, intelligent, sensitive and the epitome of good health, because you would be afraid that someone would see you as being self-centered, and all caught up with and in love with yourself. (God forbid! It's a sin for you to love yourself.) All of that is not in conjunction with the *law of harmlessness.* We must recognize our God given attributes and not diminish them. We know that thoughts are things; we know the power of the spoken word. So every time we diminish our qualities in communications because we are concerned about the reaction(s) of the individual(s) we are communicating with, we make an affirmation that comes out of our most creative chakra of all, our throat chakra. We are sending out all of this energy supported by all of our bodies in action, and we are professing our diminished state of accomplishment and abilities. We do all that out of our desire to be humble and to appear to be a humble, regular person.

Can any of us be a "regular" person? Or did we, in our quest for illumination volunteer to give up that position of being a "regular" person who follows the principles and dictates of church, cultural concepts, educational limitations, societal injections? In our quest for greater insight into the true nature of the human animal we have given up the privilege to remain in mediocrity. We must find ways to identify ourselves through the spoken word that would and could be important to the persons we communicate with. We would be informing them through a balanced understanding of what we have recognized about ourselves and are activating within ourselves, as a part and parcel of our creative opportunities. So many of us harm ourselves on a regular basis as we profess our insecurities, self-doubts and inadequacies to curry favor with the individuals in our association.

To be harmless with ourselves means that above all else we cannot commit the sin of omission, and omission is denial.

This *law of harmlessness* causes us to have to practice active listening and selective choosing, because it is within the realm of our capabilities to choose to be harmless to ourselves and thus really harmless to everyone else. That doesn't mean that we are like a steamroller and just roll over everyone else. Having been exposed to the *laws of attraction, compensation* and *cause and effect* we know that the conditions and situations we find active in our environments are of our own making and are these laws in action. We have to sort through all of the information in a harmless way so that we can balance out our responses to individuals we encounter and make situations work for us instead of us working for them.

Seeker: You said we break the *law of harmlessness* by professing our insecurities in the hope of currying favor with individuals in our association. Would you give an example of that?

Jordan: We don't make statements as a matter of fact. We make them with hope. We say, "I love you," in the hope that a person says, "I love you, too." It has been made with hope, not as a matter of fact. The statement has been said manipulatively and destructively.

It's been made out of our desire to manipulate the individual we are communicating with so that they will do for us what we don't think we are worthy of. That's very much playing the game of harmful manipulation. As the *law of compensation* begins its work and as we are dealing with the *law of cause and effect,* what we attempt to do to someone else we stand in jeopardy of having done to us.

The *law of harmlessness* does not say we have to be perfect, illuminated beings before we can communicate. It does say that our attitude and our intent and purpose should not be peppered with our desire for control and manipulation to acquire what we don't believe we have. It should be an honest evaluation of what we think, feel and are experiencing in the moment, with the realization that those feelings, thoughts and experiences can expand and show us greater dimensions of our own self. If we have broken the law we must pay the price, and we must return to confront that distorted concept of the *law of harmlessness.* If each of us would activate this law for ourselves, we would be expressing honest communications and open ourselves to a much greater opportunity to expand in our self-awareness as we are prepared and ready to work with the reactions that we encounter from the individuals we are communicating with. If I can say, "I love you, and it doesn't matter how you feel about me. I love you simply for the joy of loving because it gives me so many rewards," that would be harmless communication because we don't want to manipulate a response.

Seeker: How can I clearly recognize the difference between harmlessness and self-denial?

Jordan: Harmlessness is the realization that you have chosen everything and knowing that you can work through it through the balancing, the recognition and the application of these laws. That is harmlessness. Denial is when you express being caught up in a limited situation without having the ability to transmute it. If you are diagnosed as a schizophrenic, harmlessness would be to say, "Okay, I don't have to labor under it." Denial would be to say, "I'm schizophrenic, I have to suffer with it."

Seeker: Is it being harmless to take an animal's life force to make a fur coat out of its skin?

Jordan: How do you know that the fur didn't come from an overabundance of animals? You might have been very harmless to that race of animals by reducing the population so that the remaining animals could live a healthy life. It must be done with the proper attitude. When you are eating the meat of an animal, it must be done with the proper attitude. You are hoping that it will nourish your body and give you the strength and stamina to be able to do good things in society. Then that animal's life force has made a step up in evolution because it has merged with your life force, working inside of you hopefully exemplifying a better way of life as you go about living life. The animal and plant kingdoms are not just there for our usage. They are there to provide us with evolution, to assist in our evolution, as we provide them their evolution. It's all in how we merge with and utilize the energy. It is not a question of identifying ourselves with ownership, it is identifying ourselves as administrators, as custodians.

Non-judgment

Judgment is an encapsulation of identification that doesn't allow room for expansion or alteration. Judgment oftentimes denotes a great deal of fear as we are exposed to opportunities for expansion of our consciousness. Judgment gives us in many respects a concrete idea, which again, does not necessarily allow for expansion, alteration and change. Judgment usually encompasses all of that "unwilling" recognition of what oftentimes is active or dormant, which is waiting to be activated in our own lives. We find it really easy to make judgments about the things that we fear, the things that we have experienced, the things that we are afraid of experiencing and the things that we have an incomplete understanding of. It's so easy for us to judge those things that could be, that might exist inside of us but we haven't yet brought into manifestation. Judgment brings along limitation, encapsulation and the inability for movement, the inability for expansion.

Discernment is the ability to recognize the existing facts, the existing situations that we confront but to see beyond that existence of factual information, factual conditions and circumstances into the possibility of what can be manifested. Here is the difference between judgment and discernment. Judgment makes it absolutely concrete, immutable and unchangeable. No matter what happens, that's it. Discernment says, "This is what I see existing, this is what I see occurring, but it can alter, change and expand itself."

Let me take a situation that is well known to all of us. We feel so superior to third-world countries that we want to go in and do things for them. We want to say, "You are no good, you are inferior, so we will support you, take care of you, direct you and guide you." If we understood bridging natural law and man's law, we would know that our purpose is to educate, not to pacify. That's the difference. But we pacify everyone—our families, co-workers, friends— instead of recognizing that they are as capable of understanding as we are. We are supposed to be their teacher, but we want to prove to ourselves that we are their teacher by having them submit to our concepts and our awarenesses instead of giving them a choice. What we are actually doing is enslaving them; thus, we are out of balance with the *laws of non-judgment* and *non-force.*

I use discernment. I prefer not to spend my life in a movie theater, reading the newspaper, in a bar. I don't want to fill my brain with all that information. I prefer to recognize that we are going through a great change and a great evolutionary process. I prefer not to see you as ill and incapable human beings. I prefer to see you as very capable human beings, and it is the seeing that allows me to be capable. We discern what we see. We do not judge it. We don't particularly care for it, or we do care for it, so there are two sides, aren't there? Judgment says, "This is it, forget it, I won't be part of it." Discernment says, "I don't like this, but there has to be a way to make it better." You don't get emotionally tied into discernment; you do get emotionally tied into judgment.

It will help us to abide by the *law of non-judgment* if we use the words balanced and unbalanced in place of the words positive and negative. As soon as we say "negative" and "positive" we visualize on our mental screen pre-perceived actions, and we want to break those mental images. Balanced or unbalanced is a new attitude for us, we don't have all of these predetermined classifications.

Seeker: How do I move from an intellectual understanding into a complete understanding of non-judgment of self; like living in the moment, recognizing and being grateful for what I have accomplished, being content where I am now and not being impatient to express what is mine to express, and what is possible for me to express? How do I make that into an active action rather than an intellectual knowledge?

Jordan: By following the *law of non-judgment*. Each time we find ourselves caught in the trap of comparing and judging our personality identity, we also find ourselves being extremely critical and evaluative of the manifestations we encounter as the learning lessons that will bring us back to uniting those two bodies, the trust body and the comprehensive body. So our first step is to practice non-judgment with everything around about us. We look at everything as if we were in a third person's shoes. We see the value that exists behind and within every experience.

    You are going to say that's very difficult to do. Well, I didn't say it was easy. But the rewards will bring you into a greater sense of self-awareness, self-direction and self-realization, which is what we are all searching for. So the actual discipline is to look at every exterior circumstance we encounter non-judgmentally, and to look for the lesson there within by asking, "What are you here for? What are you showing me? Where am I going with you?" Once you have derived that information, then you can ask yourself "Do I want it?" If you don't want it, it's an experience you're done with. You have learned the lesson(s) from it, and you can release it. Then you can program what you do want through positive affirmations and positive statements. That means a total discipline of your evaluation of personality identity. It's easy once you recognize that the personality identity is not to be disposed of or denied but to be directed. Too many individuals in their evolutionary climb up Jacob's ladder of evolution want to deny the very tool that the spirit is going to use in a balanced way in order to bring about their greater communication.

Each of us is born with that still small voice, that conscience inside of us. There is absolutely no one without a conscience, without a soul, without a spirit including all of its dimensions and divisions. If you accept that without question, it will assist you in getting in touch with the existence of that conscience, that spirit, that soul, that divine energy force inside of your own self. And you will listen more clearly.

When we are not judging and comparing the outer circumstances of our recognized, our unrecognized manifestation and our subconscious creation, it makes it much easier for us to accept it, to direct it and to transmute it. Impatience comes merely because we have a lack of self-security. That lack of self-security is constantly demanding visual proofs from exterior sources of what we ourselves do not believe. If we can't believe it in us, then the next step is to see it, believe it and support it in others. As we give that support, that belief, it then acts like a boomerang—it comes back to us eventually. That's precisely the discipline. It's the acceptance through recognition of each of those personality traits and seeing how, when directed, they will be the greatest assistance we will have to expressing our true identity. Cease to deny them, but comprehend them.

It's the same as going back to the drawing board. You have a blueprint for life. You have an overall goal concept. Sometimes that overall goal concept is labeled teacher, medium, minister, wife, husband, businessman, socialite. That is your desired manifestation, your blueprint. Then you begin by drawing each of your rooms within your blueprint. That means directed energy, directed education, directed comprehension and directed purpose. You bring all of those into perspective, and you view each manifestation that you experience, via your own creations, as an opportunity to become more aware of the incomplete energy projections that you are making in this blueprint of life that you are creating. That then allows you to see the individuals that you create in your life as an expression of your dedication, your comprehension, your balance and your ability to see the details of your blueprint for life and your overall goal structure.

It is the same concept that we utilize when we are listening to our guiding forces that we in our philosophy call joy guide, Indian, chemist, doctor, inspirational teacher, master, universal master. It's a step-by-step procedure that shows us how we direct our energy patterns from our belief structure, from our emotional body, from our mental body and the unity that is there within. Remember, we've got to bring our words into harmony with our feelings. That's the great step that each of us is taking. Non-judgment of everything we encounter in life and discernment will assist us tremendously.

Seeker: I am very judgmental of my impatience. I am angry about the time I am wasting going in circles. How can I turn that judgment around?

Jordan: Stop judging and redirect. You are wasting more time by being judgmental of your impatience than if you just directed that impatience into manifestation and into being by accepting you are it. If you accept that you are a healer, a psychic, a teacher, you can direct the energy to perfecting what you are.

Seeker: If we adhere to the law of non-judgment, we don't have to be afraid of anything?

Jordan: I am just feeling the energies. I am already balanced. I am neutrality. I am magnetic. I don't have to worry about being the magnet because I am safe. By my attitude, my concept, my understanding, and my purpose I am safe. If I am practicing the *law of non-judgment* I am not afraid of anything, of any disease that is known to mankind, because I am only performing in the service of my God.

Seeker: How do we make that first step in judging ourselves?

Jordan: That's easy because we live in a competitive society without any faith. We have measured our success by our bodies and by our abilities to acquire material things. We never recognize the *law of attraction.* My success is measured by what I attract to me. "By their works shall they be known." You try to measure your success or your vision of yourself by outer trappings. You go into debt and you do all manner of things to obtain. If you were applying the *law of attraction,* you would automatically attract these things to you. You might have to work for them; you might have to discipline yourself to them; you might have to change yourself for them. In this competitive world, you can immediately, almost like a protective measure, evaluate everybody in the room to determine who is better, who is younger, who is more obedient, who is applying the laws and who is not, who is the better psychic. Your brains do. You have to discipline your brain. Acceptance. That's how you clear away the lower astral planes. That's how you begin to fulfill your karma. Up to now you have been working through everything you have absorbed and attracted to yourself, and you have done it on a daily basis.

Just start thinking limitation, you will get it right back.

Seeker: When we recognize that we've been judging or criticizing someone else's words or actions, because we weren't willing to recognize or discipline them within ourselves, how do we work with cleaning up the atmosphere?

Jordan: We clean up the atmosphere first through understanding and accepting the cause and the effect. Then we trace our insecurities. We discipline them through recognition. We use various color applications such as the ultraviolet flame, the rolling flame or the white light.

Seeker: Isn't an evaluation somehow a judgment?

Jordan: No, it isn't. An evaluation is merely looking at the outer circumstances and knowing that they can be changed through a dedicated effort. Judgment says I can't affect this, it simply is. So I run away from it. I shut the door to it, and I won't experience it.

Seeker: Where is the borderline between judgment and discernment?

Jordan: The moment you see something as unchangeable, it is a judgment. The moment you encapsulate something in your mind, you make it absolutely unchangeable. When you can discern it, you can converse with people.

You can illuminate people through your body language, emotional projection and mental reaction. You know that one part of their being is drinking in and receptive to what you are saying. You can scan your own many levels of consciousness and see if what you're discerning is active in you. When you see things as actions, habit patterns, as behaviorisms in humanity, recognize that tendency within you, whether it's active or inactive, and make selective choices. Ask yourself if you will indulge in it or discipline it. I am delighted to be able to meet and greet so many facets of myself (people) because, with discernment, I can look at what they have created in their lives. I can look at the actions in their lives. I can evaluate what of what I discern I want to put into action in my life and what I want to keep dormant in my life. That allows me freedom of choice and to walk through life not having to indulge in a lot of the experiences that you are showing me.

Seeker: What do I do when other people are judging me and it hurts me?

Jordan: It keeps you on the straight and narrow. It can't hurt you unless you want to be hurt by it; unless you are partaking in it.

Seeker: So I shouldn't care what others think about me?

Jordan: It is most important that you care what you think about you. You have to know what you are about, you have to approve of you. Nothing can touch you unless you let it. These people are only judging themselves. If your boss tells you that you are not working enough, do you know you are working enough? Are you giving your boss what you consider to be a fair exchange for your pay? You are not responsible for his recognition if you know inside that you have given him a fair exchange of your labor for what you expect to get from him. Then his view of your labor is unimportant. The worst he can do is to free you from a limiting situation which will allow you to find a better one that can be in conjunction with your evolutionary process. So why should it affect you when you are not guilty? If you know that you are doing a fair exchange you don't have to accept his "gift." You can return it unopened. Be comfortable with what you are presenting, be confident that you are living up to your contractual agreement. Then it doesn't matter what anyone else says. You can only learn from it. You learn more about your boss than he knows he is telling you. That is being constructively sensitive and being in conjunction with the laws.

Seeker: I am working very hard in my sleep state. Does that mean I am too judgmental during the day?

Jordan: You work so hard in your sleep state because you are such a perfectionist in your awake state. You're extremely judgmental in the awake state. You are battling your own feelings of inadequacies, you are stubborn, and you refuse to submit. You never submitted to your husband, to your children, to anyone, and you are extremely critical of anyone who can't see the importance of his or her own spiritual growth. That's why you work so hard on the astral plane. When you can allow people to be what they have chosen to be, and know it's all in divine order for them, then you will stop working so hard.

Non-comparison

The great ascended ones, the great magi, have said to us by their performances, their words, and their thoughts, that we too, can do the things that we witness being done. All we have to do is follow the sign posts and look realistically at the lessons we have created for ourselves in life and stop making excuses for them.

When we look back at what we were, we are actually becoming "Lot's wife." "Lot's wife" symbolizes the desire to look back and to compare. When we look back to where we started and compare it to where we are now, we are re-evoking where we started. Every time we look back we are re-evoking and recreating in a one dimensional facet of our subconscious mind those tapes that we (obviously must) have overcome in order to be where we are.

You don't compare your understanding with my understanding, your being with my being, your situation with my situation, your understanding with another person's understanding. You work with your own understanding, with your own being. You do not compare your karma with my karma. The moment you compare, you're either going to be superior or inferior in an expressional facet of your creative process.

As we listen, we are looking to explain, justify or excuse our actions. So we do not hear what people are communicating. And we have our greatest problem in maintaining our concentration because we are breaking the *law of non-comparison*. We are trying to compare the energies and activities that individuals are expressing. We want to know what they are thinking and feeling. So we send out our players in scattered directions and make ourselves totally subject to all the returning scattered energy, which is a distraction from the concentrated effort that we are supposed to be making.

When we do our deep breathing, our preparation and our goal setting, and we have done it realistically, then we can be more concentrated because we won't be sending out those players to evaluate, to compare, to determine how we're coming across to everyone else. We will be concentratively aware of listening to what we are espousing. We are aware if it is what we really want to say, to teach and to be. We won't particularly allow ourselves to be distracted by the responses of the listener or what is going on around about us.

I meditate for only one reason; for my restoration, rejuvenation and self-recognition. I don't care what's happening to you, whether you are going into an altered state of consciousness, spirit is moving your body or Indians are in there doing a pow-wow. So I can put concentrated effort into my meditation. After all, your success isn't going to mean a thing to me unless from your success you can tell me how to be more successful myself. You are entitled to your success. If I recognize your success, I am going to say to you, "Okay, I want to know what you did, when you did it, where you did it, how you did it and why you did it." Then I'm going to do it myself, and I'm not going to interpret it or change it to fit my particular situation and circumstances. I'm going to do it exactly; I'm going to be it. Concentrated, direct efforts. I pull in those players, I don't break the *law of non-comparison*. I accept the fact that I am unique and special in my own environment and should be special to myself. If I'm not special to myself, how can I possibly be special to anyone else?

Seeker: We compare ourselves to what we think we should be doing, what we could be doing because of the insecurities that we create for ourselves and because of our self-judgments and our self-limitations. How do we work with that?

Jordan: First of all, whenever you get into breaking the *law of non-comparison* you are dealing with an undisciplined psychic awareness. What you are actually doing is psychically becoming aware of your overall goal purpose; of what you could be doing, what you should be doing. And you are not happy with what you are doing. As a result you start comparing yourself to situations and circumstances and to other people. Then you break the *law of non-judgment,* and you usually end up judging yourself as being either inferior or superior. Neither one is a constructive place to be. The most beneficial way to deal with this comparison is to use it as an inspiration, with the realization that you have the same opportunities and abilities. All you have to do is learn how to put them into practice. That ignites your desire to educate yourself in whatever you see as an example in front of you. I'm not denying the reality that some individuals have spent a great deal of their life force in establishing a financial fortune. That's according to the *law of cause and effect.* And their life force or their example ignites and inspires other persons to the realization that if they want a financial fortune, it will take a certain amount of choice, discipline, direction, and obedience. They are the living teachers by their example, by demonstrating to humanity. Though they appear to be special, they are not. They just have directed their life force very one-pointedly. It is all right for you to evaluate. And there is a difference between a comparison and an evaluation. With an evaluation we open the door to what we need to do, in a self-disciplinary way, to demonstrate the same thing, because we all have it. When we start comparing we start judging. Then we are dealing with cause and effect and with the *law of harmlessness.* Then we are pushing the *law of compensation* (and the *laws of non-omission* and *non-denial*). That's when we begin to feel and think, "This one is so much better than I because look at what she's done." Not so. This one has decided that this is what she wants to be an example of in her life, which then is the encouragement. You should never hide your light under a bushel of comparison or omission because you act as an ignition switch that ignites the desire within another person. So don't compare. If what someone else has was important to you, you would have it. Look at where you are right now and learn the lesson at hand, because the choices that you've made in life, from your subconscious mind, your conscious mind and from your actions, are visible in the worlds in which you live.

Seeker: Where is the borderline between comparison and discernment?

Jordan: Comparison is when you put yourself up against someone and you feel better than or less than that person. I don't want that feeling. I don't want to have to be responsible for you and your life. It's enough to be responsible for my own. I don't want to feel that I am better than you are. So I have to see you as being equal. If you want what I've got, you'll work just as hard to get it. If you don't, you must like what you've got. Why should I compare myself? I already know that all the traits you demonstrate I've either indulged in and am disciplining at this moment, or I have activated in another lifetime and had to come to an understanding, acceptance and discipline of. Or, these traits are unrecognized and I am going to experience them, and you are showing me what not to do. So if it's not what I want, I am going to learn from you. If your life coexists with mine and they support each other, we can build a great temple of light. You can share your expertise and I can share mine, because there is no comparison, no competition.

Seeker: How do I overcome inadequacy through the application of the laws? Is it through loving myself?

Jordan: It's not only through loving yourself. You must stop comparing yourself. Take time to be who you are. If you are busy being who you are, you don't have time to compare yourself with other beings. Be grateful to be who you are, in conjunction with the laws. If you are busy being what you are, what you have seen and accepted thus far, your compensation will validate your disciplinary efforts. You will also evaluate where you need to look at the effect, get beyond the effect into the cause, which is judgment, comparison and denial.

Non-force

The *law of non-force* only works when we are completely in conjunction with the rest of the laws. Until then we will attempt to force mankind by our emotional emanations, mental descriptions, verbal accusations and physical attitudes to give us what we haven't given ourselves. Ultimately we must put the *law of non-force* into action and give to ourselves. Then we will not ask what a center, a person, a government will give us, but we will ask what we can bring to a center, a person, a government. We will not ask what marriage, love, spirit, truth or God is going to give to us, but we will ask what we can bring to it. As soon as we ask what we can bring to it, we are in conjunction with the laws. And that means we know we have it. What will we bring to wealth? It is the realization as to how we will make it grow and how we are going to direct it and use it. We will not make it a statement of our personality identity, because wealth doesn't need that statement, wealth has already its own identity.

The *law of non-force* is perhaps the most intricate and most difficult law that exists. We say "I'll love you as long as you meet all of my expectations, as long as you do everything I expect you to do. I'll work for you as long as you don't demand from me what I am unwilling to give. I'll be to you, Father God, what you want me to be, as long as you don't give me any hardship that I have to move through. I'll serve you, God, as long as I can reach out and acquire all of my personal needs and gratification from outside sources. Father God, I'll serve you as long as you provide me the income so that I can sustain all the expectations that everyone else seems to levy upon me. God, I'll serve you, I'll stay healthy, but you have to meet these requirements. I'll be true to you as long as you bring me these things."

A man looks at all the women he meets and says: "If you can eradicate all of the past experiences I've had with women, and you can sustain me in my search while I indulge my own confusions, doubts and fears, then you can have the wonderful realization that you've turned a sow's ear into a silk purse. If you can meet all my expectations, and prove to me what I don't think I am, then I'll meet a little of your expectations." Isn't that force? "I'll play your role; I'll meet your expectations as long as it suits me, as long as you are giving me what I don't think I have."

We break the *law of non-force* while we are sitting in our trance circles and deny what we encounter there, what we experience, because we are not sure it will find favor with our listeners. So we ignore it. We force ourselves not to convey what spirit is impressing on our brain. And when someone else has the guts to express it, then we say, "Oh, but I had that same impression."

I cannot force myself to accept another person

Seeker: There is a person I just can't accept as he is. I cannot just tell myself to accept him, it won't work.

Jordan: Why can't you accept him? What is he showing you about yourself that you haven't recognized or don't want to discipline?

Seeker: I have to think about that.

Jordan: That's the whole process of the natural laws. It makes us think. It makes us deal with ourselves. That's why they exist. You want to avoid getting caught up in a lot of effect? Stop right now and ask yourself why you can't accept him, what you want to prove to yourself by influencing him. If it is your child and you gave him life, that was your choice. You can't expect to live life through him. You can only expect to have done your best in your expression of life. You must release him to do his best without your judgment, your criticism and your need to fulfill yourself through him. You must come to a place where you can share life with him. You don't have to like him or to associate with him. But, you must be able to love him.

If we deny our love for another human being because we evaluate and condemn his or her actions, that's a judgment and punishment because we create an encapsulation. The premise upon which we love all humanity is that people, including ourselves, are an extension of the creator of all. So we love them as that extension. We don't have to like their performance, their expression. That's discernment and the art of harmlessness. I don't have to like your stubbornness, but I have to love your Christed being, your God being. So I will bypass your stubbornness and love your Christ, your God being. I will not judge you but I will discern whether I want to endure your stubbornness. That's my right and my choice. And I do not break the natural laws, I am in conjunction with them.

Here is another example: A woman just died of cancer. She disliked her husband and wanted to punish him for what she thought he had done to her. She didn't have to like her husband, but she had to love him. In her last breaths she had to express love and forgiveness and take responsibility for her own suffering, because she chose to live with her dislike out of her own fears, self-judgments and limitations.

The world doesn't have to like its state of existence; it does have to love its opportunity to learn, grow, evolve, ascend and be. We don't have to like our circumstances, but we have to love ourselves through the opportunity of producing our way out of them.

The law of non-force and the opening of the chakras

Seeker: What would happen if we break the *law of non-force* to stimulate premature chakra opening?

Jordan: If you use force in the stimulation and premature awakening or opening of a chakra point so that you can gain what you think is a greater insight, that information still has to be filtered through your brain consciousness, your brain matter. It isn't going to bypass your brain matter. So here you are using force to open and awaken the chakras to affect the natural laws, and here you've got a fraction of your brain that's dead because it refuses to accept a premise that has not been proven by you personally. So you distort the whole information, and you make it extremely personalized and very limited. What good was all of your forcible chakra stimulation? If you don't believe you are spirit living in a structure, and it's your job to master the structure, then how are you going to open your visual sensory being so that you can actually experience spirit in its frequency form?

How the Natural Laws interact – Examples

Cast your bread upon the water
Harmlessness, compensation, attraction, non-judgment, non-force

Cast your bread upon the water and be harmless to yourself. Know that you are compensated by your thoughts, words and actions. Know that you have attracted into your life everything that is going to teach you and show you to yourself. Don't judge it, but understand it, recognize it and discipline it. Don't be forceful by playing a game with your brain and trying to pretend to be what you believe you are not. Don't force it; practice the *law of harmlessness,* and to the best of your ability, try not to put anything in its way.

Communicative access to our bodies
Attraction, non-judgment, non-comparison

In our associations, we have attracted to ourselves everything that represents every facet of us. We might as well look at it non-judgmentally or non-comparatively because if we compare what is happening in our environment with what we think is happening in our interior, we are going to come up either on top of the ladder or at the bottom of the ladder. Either way is not in balance and our physical, emotional and mental bodies are not communicating, and we want to have communicative access to all of our bodies. If we have communicative access to our bodies, then we'll have communicative access to the bodies of the individuals that we meet and encounter on our sojourn in life.

A new job
Non-comparison, non-judgment

When you first take a job and enter into the company with anticipation, you want everybody to like you, and you're hoping that you're going to like everybody. You pray that you learn all the techniques. You discipline yourself to activate these techniques interiorly and you create success. You function well in your job. But then you start comparing. You compare the work you're doing with the work your co-worker is doing. You compare the amount of money you are getting with the amount of money your co-worker is getting. You compare what you are earning and how much profit the boss is making. Then all of a sudden you are sending out a static energy flow. So you lose all of your interior self-recognition. You get distracted in your daily administration of your energy and you project all manner of disruptive energy out into the atmosphere, which is supported by other disruptive, unhappy energies, and you have a disruptive office environment rather than a balanced supportive environment.

You have to use your basic intelligence to select what is necessary and primary to your life at that moment in time, and to activate and master it. That means you've got to look at your self-judgment and your comparison. You've got to say, "Hello dear friend, I can't hate you because you are a part of me. I can't fear you, because that's fearing myself. I've got to learn how to communicate with you, how to administrate you, and how to use you constructively for my blueprinted plan that I have manifested." That means you've got to do some active listening. Listen clearly to your three bodies' communication. Set your priorities, use your selective choice wisely, and determine how you're going to make your outer statement, which reflects your interior recognition.

Guilt
Compensation, non-judgment, non-comparison, attraction

If you are working with guilt, you know you have been wrong. You work with the *law of compensation* and know that you have been totally undisciplined, and if you are undisciplined, you are the only one who suffers. Isn't that why we have healers? They help to ease the dis-ease that brought on the pain. Then they must educate. The pain is to be gone forever. That's why we have healers, teachers, mediums, music therapists, color therapists, etc., etc.

Guilt is a by-product of self-judgment and a refusal to gain self-understanding. I don't like many things, but I don't feel guilty about anything. That is the difference between judgment and discernment. But I won't live with these things. My discernment says, "I am not responsible for others, but I will attempt to educate them." There is a vast difference. What is negativity? You all have this concept that negativity is some evil force that is out to get you. You have been living by man's laws for so long that you have been "getting" yourself. No one else ever had to go out and deliberately try to make you miserable, you have done that yourselves. You have accepted man's laws by your self-judgment, your comparison and by working the *law of attraction*. You attract those situations to yourselves, don't you? When you finally accept that you are God and recognize the *law of compensation* and the natural laws, then you will be able to work with them.

It isn't so much that you are unwilling to know yourself as much as you are unwilling to discipline yourself, and if you work at it, then you have no excuse not to discipline it. As long as you profess ignorance, you are able to continue to indulge in your own self-destruction.

Compensation versus cause and effect

We are dealing with the necessity for us to assume priorities with the total faith and belief that, as we put forth the energy in the physical dimension to do God's will, to subject man's will to God's will, we will reach through the *law of compensation* into the *law of cause and effect*. The *law of compensation* deals with this life. The *law of cause and effect* deals with past lifetimes and associations on this earth plane.

For example: For you (a student sitting in class) it is easy to be in medicine, in all phases of it. What is difficult for you is to be in philosophy and all phases of it. Your karma, which is the *law of cause and effect*, keeps continuously motivating you to enter into philosophy and metaphysics. No matter how many degrees you get in medicine—that is easy for you, you mastered that from the Atlantean period—you are now here to deal with the *law of compensation* and the *law of cause and effect*, because it says that from being balanced in your outer actions, mental associations and emotional coagulation, you will open a vortex into the *law of cause and effect*, which will allow you to then eradicate some of the imbalances from a past lifetime, which you actually came into this densification to work with.

It is easy for Susan to be a builder. She was a builder in the Atlantean period. For her those numerological and structural concepts are easy to grasp. It's like water falling off a duck's back. Her difficulty is applying them in a spiritual direction because of her self-doubt. That is brought into greater perspective when she looks at the *law of compensation* and sees what she is manifesting in her exterior environment.

For Gail it is very easy to be a mother and a wife and to submerge her own personality, which is not Italian, into an ethnic Italian background. But the minute she begins to pursue beyond that imagery she must deal with the *law of cause and effect*.

It is easy for some of you to respond as women even though you are men in disguise, because that's your *law of compensation* in action. But when you deal with your masculinity and your need to control and manipulate everything, then you are dealing with the *law of cause and effect*, and you've moved into another frequency of completion and opportunity. When you're moving into the *law of divine order,* you're moving into the clairvoyant concept. This means that you've brought a clear vision and a clear understanding of what you are creating through the *law of compensation.*

Lucy knows that as long as she paints her face, does her hair and keeps her body youthful, she can generate enough money as a cocktail waitress to keep herself satisfied and to fulfill her action of the *law of compensation* in balance. It is when she recognizes that as a cocktail waitress she can also emanate spirituality that she moves into a recognition of herself, into a cause and effect frequency, and touches the souls of those individuals she has known in a past life. That's how it works.

It is easy for Jim to be a salesman. He sold religion to many people back in Greece and Egypt as a priest in the temples of Egypt. He served the God Ra. The *law of compensation* will show him where his thinking and his emotions are out of balance, which then shows up in his physical life. As a result, it is when he begins to recognize that his selling of plants and flowers produces a balancing effect on the people who buy them, and he sees into that aspect of the *law of compensation* in action that he begins to work with his responsibility to project his spirituality into his selling. He then incorporates the frequency of cause and effect into the frequency of compensation.

It is easy for Jerry to be a money consultant because he was a tax collector in Israel. But he abused his power in this role. So the *law of compensation* says that he will be a male, that he will deal with his femininity, and that he will look to all the outer manifestations of approval to prove that he is a male instead of a female. Then he will begin to express his expertise in financial management. As he begins to apply spirituality, he creates a vortex into the *law of cause and effect.* He doesn't just deal with compensation in this lifetime, but he begins to incorporate past lifetimes into what he's experiencing in this lifetime. As a result it then compounds and creates more need for self-control, self-understanding, self-discipline and self-motivation. This is exactly what Paramahansa Yogananda came to teach.

That's what we're dealing with when we talk about the *law of cause and effect*. You rarely get to the *law of cause and effect* until you understand the *law of compensation*.

Linda's husband is a reflection of the *law of compensation* in action.

Laura's boyfriends are a reflection of the *law of compensation* in action. And it is only when she brings this realization into balance will she begin to see her karmic indebtedness with them.

Richard's wife is his karma. But only when he deals with the *law of compensation* will he be able to open the vortex to understand what karma caused him to associate with her in this lifetime, and vice versa.

The *law of compensation* says that we attract, according to our physical, mental and emotional emanations of existing energy into the physical dimension, those persons, experiences and happenings that cause us to take a look at ourselves and our fears of self-exposure. That's the greatest fear that we fear. Poverty, spiritual lack, a lack of control are states of consciousness, and we must experience in this physical dimension what we're putting out and vacillating on.

Cindy called and said, "I want to come out and see your mother." The motivation was cause and effect. The fear of the highway and ice on the road, the fear of a rented car, and the fear of danger was compensation. So she attracted an accident and an illness. Whereas if she had opened up to a higher frequency and said, "My purpose is to bring light and love to somebody I love. I am going to be safe, and I am going to accomplish my mission," that would have brought her more insight into her past association with my mother, who was her mother in a Greek incarnation. When she recognizes that, it will begin to allow her to apply a greater understanding in her association with her mother and father in this lifetime. It all correlates. You are too hung up in your being black, Italian, Jewish and so forth, just as I was totally hung up in my aristocratic German heritage, but I have disciplined myself not to be hung up in it a long time ago.

Healing
Non-judgment, cause and effect

I know all these wonderfully educated individuals. They've spent many weekends and many years reading and learning how to use some form of healing. They are Reiki masters, Aura Soma masters, foot reflexology masters. They go through all these physical procedures of doing all this wonderful touch healing and sending all this fabulous God energy through their patient. When the patient gets off the table they look at him and ask: "Don't you feel better?" As soon as they do that they've reactivated their original diagnosis, their original vision of the discomfort that existed in the patient, which they just magnetically pulled out. So the patient looks at them and says: "Well, I feel something but I'm not healthy, I'm still sick." So these healers start judging what's wrong with their technique, with their ability and wonder why their patient wasn't instantly healed. Instead they should look at it as a piece of information leading them to the realization that, according to the *law of cause and effect*, the patient wasn't ready or willing to give up the cause that was bringing about the effect. The patient was using the effect to beat his family and to affect his society in an accusatory action that says, "Look and see what you have made me. Now feel guilty because you did it to me." That is information and should lead healers to a place where they determine how they're going to do positive reinforcement instead of negative reconstruction, and get the patient to come to terms with the *law of cause and effect*.

Life's daily annoyances
Non-judgment, non-comparison

We get ourselves together, hustle out the door being unhappy with our woman because the eggs were too hard, our shoes weren't polished and the kids were screaming. So we are a little bit disgruntled with her and we project all of these horrible vibrations about what we may be confronting as we walk through the door of our office. All of a sudden our boss looks at us and says, "You didn't finish yesterday's reports, what is wrong with you?" We become shocked and totally out of balance because we instantly judge that he doesn't like us, that we can never do anything to make him happy. But the poor old fellow is only trying to convey to us that he is having a hard time. His woman just ran the Mercedes through the garage door, the kids are at each other's throats, his mother-in-law is coming to live with them permanently. So he is not in a very receptive mood, and is conveying a necessity for us to do some active healing, some active education, through our projections and visualization; and not to take his accusation personally. But if we hadn't done comparison and judgment, we wouldn't have taken it so personally and would have gotten down to the nitty-gritty of what the old fellow was really saying.

Meeting ourselves
Attraction, non-judgment

According to the *law of attraction,* we meet both the good and the bad of our personality. With everyone we encounter in the work place, at home, in the family, in the social place, we are meeting ourselves. And we get a view of what we can choose to be. I learned the greatest lesson when I elected to go into prisons to teach astral projection. I came to the realization that I was meeting myself in every prisoner that was behind bars. I realized that I could choose to commit, at any moment, whatever crime each of the prisoners had committed. I, too, could choose to perpetrate that same malfunction in any moment. I could choose to be a murderer, a thief, an abuser, a misuser if it wasn't for my attachment to my principle. It is my principle that keeps me from doing those things. But I can be it. It brought me to realize that I've been the murderer every time I've taken someone's freedom of expression away because I've judged it, gossiped about it, condemned it. I've certainly broken the *law of non-judgment,* and I am still tempted to do it. But it is my choice. We meet our personalities. I've been angry, I can be angry again. So when I meet angry people I know that I've seen my personality. We see ourselves coming and going.

Karma and self-limitations
Non-comparison, non-judgment, compensation, divine order

We were meant to experience joy, happiness and a garden of Eden. But we don't. We experience turmoil on a universal scale, governmental scale, educational scale, family scale and individual scale. All of this is the karma that we want to change. That's the whole concept of karma. We have the dharma, the God being, inside of us that says, "You can, you will and you must," but then we break the *laws of non-comparison and non-judgment.* We compare ourselves with everybody and we judge what we have experienced in the past. So we constantly deny ourselves. That is visible in the amount of money, love and pleasure we have. Somehow, somewhere we must come to a place where we recognize that it is we who are limiting ourselves. We have to stop blaming family, education and society for where our limitations are. That requires building a bridge between natural law and man's law, because unfortunately we have assimilated our identity, our whole being and concept, from man's law. We have to understand that we get back what we actually think about ourselves. That is the *law of compensation.* We have to look at what we created. We have to know that we and no one else created it. Then we have to look at the *law of divine order* and see that if we created an imbalance, if we bought self-limitations, it is neither good nor bad. It is; and we must realize that each situation gives us an opportunity to look at the lessons to be learned from each experience.

A seeker's life story—an example of the interaction of laws

Compensation, cause and effect, attraction, non-judgment, non-comparison, love, harmlessness, etc.

Seeker: I grew up in a home for foundlings and feel as though no one ever understood me. I don't have graduation papers. I was labeled and encapsulated, but I have an I.Q. of 133. My father was an alcoholic. I have six brothers and sisters. And I have never been accepted.

Jordan: The fact that you were a foundling, or you grew up in a home for foundlings, was certainly a wonderful balancing of karma. It truly gave you the opportunity to employ understanding to all the rest of the children, and to be able to see how their given situations could produce particular actions. The fact that you may even have experienced some abuse at the hands of your caretakers certainly can cause you—with an understanding heart—to feel the mental and emotional plight of those individuals who, with supposedly loving parents, have experienced physical and mental abuse. The fact that your father was addicted to a stimulant can certainly give you tools by which—without judgment, but with discernment—you can get to the cause and the reason of that addiction, rather than just getting caught into the judgment of the addiction. As a result, you might be able to help hundreds of thousands of people. The fact that you have a very high I.Q., that you have this brilliant intelligence and all these abilities, can assist you to direct yourself using understanding and discernment to assist the rest of humanity. After all, you've been balancing your scales of indebtedness since birth, and now you are having this fabulous opportunity.

I wouldn't worry so much about whether the world understood me, I think I would worry whether I understood the world. That's a thought that you might want to keep with you. It really isn't so important that the world understands you as it is that you understand the world.

Now, how can you treat yourself and each other in a more loving and balanced way? First of all by not judging yourself.

One of the greatest necessities for us to use discernment and to practice the action of discernment, is to not judge ourselves. It seems to be pretty much human nature that we usually transfer our fears and our anxieties on other people. Then we see our fears and anxieties being enacted by those individuals we most predominantly associate with. The young gentleman told me that no one in the world understands him. I wonder if he can tell me that he understands the world.

Well, young man, you might just have proven my theory that you really are judging other people, and that's why you feel judged.

Seeker: I have always been judged, no matter where I went.

Jordan: Have you been judged first, or have you judged first?

Seeker: No, I haven't. But I also have to say that I am an alcoholic, too.

Jordan: I understand that. I wonder how much you actually practice the art of discernment and how much you practice judgment. I wonder how much we all practice this art. I wonder how many of us walk down the street and when we see a fat lady say, "Look how fat she is, look how disgruntled she is" and we feel so superior because there is someone a little fatter than we are. Then we see a gentleman walking down the street with his wife and we look and we say, "How can he have such a beautiful wife?" What do you think that is? Is that judgment or is that discernment?

That's a very real characteristic I just drew for you. We look at a wealthy individual and we immediately judge him as being either better or superior to us or having had more opportunities than we've had. Isn't that a judgment? We never discern what energies it took—directed in a one-pointed way—for him to acquire that wealth. We never bother to discern what other sacrifices he has made in order to accumulate this commodity, while we've been out there enjoying sex, movies, escapism, self-destruction, or our family responsibilities, ensuring that we have indulged all the things we have wanted to. But we immediately judge that this particular individual is absolutely special and that God has favored him above everyone else.

Whereas if we were practicing discernment, we would look at this individual with this great display of wealth and say, "Oh, how marvelous. I want to discover what he did, how he has directed his thoughts and his actions, to manifest all that I see him displaying." We would look at the fat lady walking down the street and we would say, "Oh, my God, there by the grace of God go I." We would discern the fact that this fat lady is pacifying herself with food as opposed to recognizing herself and confronting her situations and altering her shape.

We would see these naughty children who are displaying temperament and instead of judging them as naughty, we would discern that they are asking for attention. We would discern that they are looking for some sort of recognition and guidance; that they are angry because they decided that they were inadequate. We would discern that they had done some comparison that caused them to become less than they had hoped or desired to be. We would see it in a much broader, not encapsulating, form.

Now, we all practice judgment. I remember the first time I went to work in an institution devoted to educating individuals—but not really to educate, because the administrators of this institution really only wanted baby sitters—who were suffering from supposed brain damage, from multiple sclerosis and all kinds of physical limitations. Most of society had judged them as being inadequate and inferior. So these individuals responded with feelings of inferiority. Well, I thought, "What in the world can I really teach these people? They're brain damaged. They're physically impaired. They certainly can't do all the activities that are necessary." When I got into the institution, I left my particular society with all of its formations and expectations of behaviorism and of identification as to what is normal, what is abnormal, what is good, what is bad. I was in a society where I was the only abnormal creature because I was walking on my two feet and able to move myself, not in a wheel chair but under my own power. I finally realized that I had walked in there with a preconceived, judged attitude of their inferiority and that I had geared all of my reactions to this preconceived, judged identification. Then I began to learn the difference between judgment and discernment. I saw young men and women in various different degrees of physical deformity performing tasks.

One young man wrote me the most beautiful poem I've ever received in my life, but it took him six months, because he wrote with a pencil between his teeth and moving his neck. He simply wrote, "Please tell the world not to judge us, but to discern us. To see that our physical condition doesn't impair our mind; that our physical conditions, our mental conditions don't limit our soul recognition. We're tired of being judged and limited when all we need is some encouragement, some patience, some enlightenment and some tender care." That taught me a lot about judgment. It taught me to be able to discern a situation, and in the discernment recognize that if I can find the right particular cure, the right particular incentive, any discerned unbalanced energy or action can be altered and changed if the individual wants it so.

It's learning to be able to live and cope with the presence of the realities of life. Most of us have our greatest problem because we judge other individuals' reactions to us, and we judge ourselves, if the reaction is not favorable, as being inadequate. We never bother to consider whether that particular individual or group of individuals of themselves, by themselves are not moving through their own problematic situations, which don't involve us at all. But we make such snap judgments because we are working with our very limited concept of what is right and what is wrong. What's right and what's wrong is determined by each and everyone of the statements that we want to make of ourselves according to some basic guidelines that our society determines as acceptable behavior. I said "acceptable behavior," I didn't say "right behavior" or "wrong behavior." So we govern ourselves in those basic, fundamental expressions according to what's acceptable, what we know we can get by with without having to pay an extreme price. But what's right for you may not be right for me; what's good for you may not be good for me. If I judge a man's actions and I say, "He is a self-destructive, over-angry, pseudo-intellect who is feeling sorry for himself and wants to punish the whole world, so he is punishing himself by hating everybody in the world and feeling rejected by the whole world," then I might limit his ability to move into greater self-recognition and into greater self-acceptance. By my judgment I might limit his ability to communicate in a more balanced way with people.

That is if I was going to do judgment. But if I'm to do discernment, I'm going to say, "He's a very injured young man who hasn't recognized all the magnificent things that God gave him to compensate for the balancing of the karmic scales with his parental influence and with his societal influence." Then I might ask him to come up here. Are you willing to do that? (Seeker: Yes.) If I had a mirror, I might let you stand in front of it and I might say, "Look at yourself. You've got a fairly attractive face. You're not wearing any scars, not outwardly anyway, maybe inwardly. You've got two eyes to see, a high level of intelligence, a fairly movable body. You've got all your parts and they're put together okay." So God really gave you compensation for all of the emotional and intellectual traumas that you went through. Now what would you like to do with it? (Seeker shows his tattoos.) Oh, but these are self-inflicted. The body still is fabulous. You do have a foot, a kneecap, a thigh, don't you? Now you could be without one of those body parts. Then you would have something to cry about. May I touch you? (Seeker: Yes.) Close your eyes. Do they function? (Seeker: Yes.) You can see through them? Oh, well, you might be without them. Go sit down and cry on someone else's shoulder.

My dear friend, you haven't discerned the situation and asked yourself what you want to do about it. You have judged the situation, and you are professing your anger at how you have evaluated that situation and what it means. You are giving yourself a perfect excuse to stagnate in your own superiority because the bottom line is that according to your own admission, you've got an almost brilliant mind, a very good body and all of the qualities except self-respect and self-belief.

We are working on judgment, discernment, understanding, and how we can communicate in a more balanced and less threatening and less limiting way with each other. When we stop judging ourselves, and we stop limiting ourselves in the situations we find ourselves involved in, we ask ourselves through discernment "What do I want to do about it? How do I want to cope with what I'm learning here? How do I want to turn this all around so I can use it beneficially, or constructively, to assist other people who are frightened and insecure and who don't know what they've got as tools by which they can affect the world? What do I want to do about this situation?" If you would answer, "These are the facts: I grew up with an alcoholic father. I was deserted by my mother. I was raised in an orphanage. I was mistreated by the caretakers. And as soon as I could buy a drink, I went out and followed in my father's footsteps. I became an alcoholic myself so that I, too, could tell the world to go to hell," that would be a judgment.

Discernment leaves the door open for us to change the situation. If we can't change the situation, we can change our perspective of it. When we don't get caught in good and bad, devil and angel, we can look at the situation and say, "It's not what I want for me. If it makes you happy and you're contented in it, be my guest. But I don't intend to live in it, under it or with it."

Seeker: I am not just dependent on alcohol, I am also dependent on my wife. This afternoon she locked the door so that I couldn't get out.

Jordan: Maybe your wife is afraid you're going to leave her. (Seeker: Yes) You probably will if you ever decide to be harmless to yourself. Why are you so dependent on your wife? For financial support? For cooking?

Seeker: No, for sexual gratification.

Jordan: But you really don't have to be dependent on her. So, obviously you want to be dependent on her. You are gratifying this need for self-punishment, but you are a lovely young man and you've got your whole life in front of you. Now what do you want to do about this situation? You have judged that you are dependent on this woman for sexual gratification. You mean there is no other woman on this earth plane that would participate in sexual gratification with you?

Don't think that I'm just talking to this young man. I am talking to everybody. I counsel women every day who are totally dependent on their husbands. They say it's for financial reasons, for emotional reasons, or they'll admit it's for sexual reasons or societal reasons. I counsel people who are dependent on society's approval. They wouldn't dare be themselves or even look at themselves, because their mothers, their fathers, their friends wouldn't approve.

No one is laughing at you (some people in class were laughing), so don't shut down. Let them laugh at themselves, because all you're doing is exposing their dependencies and showing them their judgments. And it's not about the world, it's about themselves. They just haven't recognized it yet. God says, according to the Holy Scriptures: Thou shall not judge. That's a very strong commandment. He does say we can discern, avoid evil, avoid self-destruction and that we should not put ourselves in jeopardy, but he also says: Thou shall not judge, least you'll be judged. Most of the people in the world judge everyone and then they complain because they have to work through their own judgment. Whereas if they could discern, they could then redirect their energies and ask: "What do I want to do about the situation?" Now I am asking you what you want to do about your situation.

Seeker: I would like to separate from my wife, but I have a five-year-old boy.

Jordan: Take him with you.

Seeker: I am not allowed to.

Jordan: Then see him on the weekends. I would not sacrifice my life for a five-year-old boy. I wouldn't sacrifice my life for a one-year-old child, and if that's the excuse you are using, I would like to ask you if you have thought of the pain and misery you are creating for this five-year-old child by the vibrations that exist between you and your wife?

Seeker: There is only tension.

Jordan: How much do you love this five-year-old child?

Seeker: Very much.

Jordan: Then love him enough to do what is best for him. Do you know how you can do what is best for him? By doing what is best for you. Because one day he is going to follow in your footsteps like you followed in your father's. Then you'll look at God and shake your finger and ask, "Why have you forsaken me?" But God has given you every opportunity to be whatever you can envision yourself to be, to take all the talents that you can discern about yourself, to look at the situations you are living in and under and to ask yourself if you like them. And if you don't like them God is giving you the opportunity to ask yourself what you can do about them, what you want to do about them. What gratifications, what excuses, and what justifications are you using as you wallow in your judgments, in your limitations, in all of your encapsulations? An individual who is blind doesn't have much of a problem in recognizing that he is sightless through the physical eyes. Now that's a judgment. But he can then discern that he has other abilities, and if he explores them, he can see with them.

I have worked with "Blind Awareness." It's an organization dedicated to assisting people who are without sight to learn to see. They see through their sensory feeling, and they can determine densified objects. They can also hear sounds that you can't possibly hear. Suppose you judge yourself as having a heart attack or heart problems. Now discern it. Look at the information and say, "What do I want to do about it?"

I'm going to tell you a story. I had a student, he was a man of about 45 years of age. He didn't like his wife, and he hated his profession. He wanted to become a spiritual being. He studied all kinds of religions, but he was constantly dealing with frustration. He judged himself as being trapped in a situation that he couldn't break free from. So he had a heart attack. They took him to the hospital and he had open heart surgery.

As science has begun to prove, when we are under the anesthetics and our spiritual body is released from its imprisonment in our physical body, we oftentimes get greater information. This student discovered how he had judged himself, how he had limited himself and how he was blaming his wife and his profession. He was actually using them to cover his fear of exploration, of going out into the world and starting over new and using all of his talents. His wife was at his bedside and he said, "Will you go and get me a picture of a perfect heart?" He was lying in his bed, his arms could just move ever so slightly because they were all tubed, and he took this picture of a perfect heart and laid it right over his incision, right over the bandages and the stitches. He said, "Heart, here is what you should look like. Here is how you should beat. I'm not going to judge anymore. I'm going to see what I can do about my life." And in 48 hours he was on his way to getting out of the hospital. He had changed his life completely. He recognized how he had enslaved himself in a judgment, how he had limited himself because his wife wasn't going to hold him, to enslave him. She was willing to let him go, if that's what made him happy. His profession was willing to let him go, if that's what made him happy. But he had judged himself because of financial reasons, educational reasons, societal expectations, and so on—he had created those concrete chains that bound him to his old performances and self-destructions.

What have you learned from your situations? What have you learned from the conditions, circumstances and situations that you have judged and evaluated as being conditions? Never lose hope or trust in the power of God almighty and in the power of your own being because when you recognize that it is a situation that you do not like, you no longer have to endure it. Too many of us are waiting for God to forgive us instead of us forgiving ourselves because Scriptures say that God can't look on evil, that he doesn't know evil. But man does. From every walk of life man knows evil, and man surely blames poor, old God for all of his self-inflicted misery. Well, when you finally do your penance and you have forgiven yourself, then you can use discernment and start working on asking yourself what you want to do about your situations.

It's so easy to compare. Shall I give you a simple, realistic discipline that you can do so you can stop judging yourself and thus stop judging other people? Okay, at your earliest convenience go into your private quarters, and stand in front of a full length mirror. Strip off all your clothes, examine every part of your body, and decide what you like about it and what you don't like about it. Then ask yourself what you really want to do about it because you have the power to do it.

Then sit down and make a list of all the educational processes you have exposed yourself to and the ones that you would like to expose yourself to, the ones that you know you haven't exposed yourself to and start doing something about it. Then go to your own administration of your time and your energy and see how many times you allow yourself to be distracted while you are feeling superior to other people and trying to do it for them instead of showing them how to do it for themselves. You will find that you have a lot of time when you stop doing it for them just so you can strengthen your superiority and encourage their inferiority.

A perfect love is a love that just is. It doesn't own; it isn't gratified because it is. Love just is. It doesn't have expectations, it has fulfillment. It doesn't own and it doesn't possess, and it is not owned by or possessed by. Perfect love says: I'm okay, you're okay. How can we communicate? How can we share? I can recognize you're suffering, but you don't need to. Whatever your circumstances have been, you don't need to suffer. You can be all that you want to be, but you're being what you've judged yourself to be.

Look at your situations realistically. Don't ask what your wife, your husband, your mother, your father is going to do about your situations, ask what you are going to do about them. When our mothers and fathers leave us, and they move to another dimension and we feel this tremendous separation, our separation is only because we have created it so. God has promised life eternal and life can always communicate in prayer and in love. If you can forgive your mothers and your fathers who have gone on, you can communicate with them. My father died in my arms. My mother died in my home and one and a half hours after her death I went and conducted a Sunday service because that's what she would have wanted me to do. I loved her because I loved myself. I accepted my parents because I accepted myself. And they have never left me because there was never a break in our communication. Their bodies may be buried, but their souls live. That's a promise that we all have. If you feel lonely, ask yourself why you are depriving yourself of your parent's presence. My mother goes with me wherever I am, and my father is always with me although I know logically that they both died in my presence. But since I'm so much a part of them and they are a part of me and we are all a great part of God, how can there be a separation?

When will you stop judging yourself as being separated from your heavenly Father? He doesn't know your weaknesses, your escapism, your limitation. He only knows you as his most perfect creation. You know yourself with all of your imperfection, and only you can change your imperfection. Your Father only knows you as his perfect creation. So who has separated from whom? My father and I—and I'm speaking about my earthly father—are not separated. His body is gone, but we are not separated. Are you separated from those you have loved? If you have loved them, how can you be? Isn't it time you forgive yourself? If you forgive yourself, and you stop judging yourself, but you discern yourself, then you can understand yourself. You can find the cause of your mental, emotional and physical malfunction, and you can start correcting it. Then you can communicate. You can communicate from your heart instead of your brain.

I'd rather see a sermon any day than hear one. I don't want people to talk at me, I want them to talk with me. I don't want someone to tell me how great she is, I want her to show me how great she is. I am not impressed with how great you tell me you are. I watch to see how great you are, how brilliant you are, and how evolved you are. Don't tell me a sermon, show me a sermon. And show yourself one. That's the most important thing. Whatever you do, don't do it for me do it for yourself. You must do it for you, always for you, because you are all God's special children. He created you with tender loving care. That love does not dissipate; it doesn't go away. You may experience pain in this life, you may experience disappointment; but the one thing you can hold on to is that God loves you. And when you love yourself the rest of the world will follow suit and love you. But you must stop judging and limiting your-self. You must say, "I can, I will, I am," and when you don't want to, don't say that your husband won't let you, your fi-nances won't let you; say that you don't want to. That's real-ism, and it is not denying your own God love. Be honest with yourself. If you are never honest with anyone else, be honest with yourself. God loves you, and you should love yourself. His love will never die.

Real communication begins with discernment, not judgment. Gossip is part of judgment, so don't gossip. Find something beautiful in everyone because in everyone is something beau-tiful. Assist yourself by exemplifying what's beautiful in every-one.

We can never overcome anything if we judge it as a punish-ment, as a reflection, as an existing lack within us. You would be surprised how many of you have said: I'm not loved be-cause I'm not pretty enough, because I don't have enough bo-som, because my legs are not long enough. You would be sur-prised how many of you have said: I'm not loved because I'm too fat. But the reality is that you are not loved because you don't want to be. You are afraid of the responsibility of being loved and you are afraid of loving yourself. As a result you are not loved. You would be surprised how many of you will sit across from me in a consultation and say: I'm incapable of doing God's work because I have a knee problem, because I have a husband, because I have children, because I have a prac-tice. Those are all your self-imposed limitations. God's work can be done in any place, under any physical circumstance. So obviously you have broken the *law of non-judgment.*

Part Three

Frequently Asked Questions

Natural laws in general

Seeker: Have the natural laws always been in existence, and when did the splitting of the atom start?

Jordan: The natural laws were in existence when God created man or when man created God.

The splitting of the atom started when man broke his association with his unity in God in order to find independent recognition. The stars, the birds, the flowers, the trees, the animals are not looking for independent recognition. They work as a unit, as part of the body; they perform a service. In the time of Atlantis, Lemuria and Mu we were contented to function and to perform a service, to be a part of the body. We didn't need to clarify whether we were the toe nail; we knew that the toe couldn't be protected without its nail. We were contented to be the nail on the toe until it was necessary for us to be the kneecap that surrounded the knee bone. This means that whatever you have chosen, function in it.

Seeker: In Atlantis they lived in accordance with natural laws.
         As they split away from their God identity, they needed
         man-made laws?

Jordan: Yes. We as a people, as uncontrolled and as undisci-
         plined as we are, require some sort of a set regimenta-
         tion that we can follow. When we did split away from
         the total utilization of natural laws we began to judge
         ourselves, and thus we developed our concepts, our
         understanding of the natural laws that brought about
         the Ten Commandments. Then within each society
         the laws were developed which have been enforced
         by man's consciousness to bring about some sort of a
         cohesive living structure.

Seeker: In the beginning there was just natural law? After we
         separated ourselves, it became a remembrance by our
         comprehension of the natural law and man's law. Is
         that correct?

Jordan: That is true. We have attempted to individualize,
         analyze, and dissect the natural laws rather than sim-
         ply obeying them. As a result we have bastardized the
         laws, and our lives reflect it.

Seeker: How did man discover the natural laws?

Jordan: Through trial and error. Just as we are able to evalu-
         ate our adherence to the Ten Commandments through
         trial and error, our physical, emotional and mental
         lives are a reflection of our awareness, understanding
         and application of the natural laws.

Seeker: Let's say I am in harmony with the natural laws, and
         I am perfect. So any communication or argument with
         my environment would become unnecessary. What
         would then be the purpose of my existence?

Jordan: Then you would be the healer, the teacher, the way-
         shower. You would elect to go into disharmonious cir-
         cumstances to radiate your wonderful education, peace
         and understanding so that you could ignite that spark
         of desire in those fragmentations of yourself. That's
         the purpose of your being. Now if your environment
         has also changed, then you will be living in utopia,

and that's precisely what we are all looking for. Utopia just wants that you see utopia everywhere. So you travel to the rest of the world to teach. You will be busy.

Seeker: Why aren't we aware of the natural laws from the very beginning, from the moment we are born?

Jordan: We are. We are actually aware of everything. But before we descended through the atmosphere we agreed to experience prearranged conditions according to our karmic/dharmic necessities. But we are aware. It is only when we get into this earth plane and are faced with the solidifications of our karmic purposes in their dense form, with our parental influence, our extended family influence and the influences of our society and geographical location that we chose to incarnate into that we begin to block out or to overcoat this emanation of understanding that we have oftentimes called conscience. So in our approach to the natural laws we have a choice to either use them in a constructive manner or to create various learning lessons that will help us to come into a greater sense of purpose and identity.

We begin to justify our indulgences. With each justification and intellectualization we actually nullify or lessen the effects of the light that we call conscience as it permeates its truth from within us. That's why I have repeatedly said that nothing is done unconsciously, that there is a conscious realization of everything that we do, say and manifest on an instantaneous basis. But we do so willingly and deliberately because of our own self-evaluations, comparison and judgments in the illusions that we create around ourselves. That means we are not living in harmony with the *law of harmlessness,* and we are most harmful to our own self-evolution. We are creating all these pitfalls on the earth plane that look like valleys and mountains that we have to climb before we reach this ascending period of understanding and can begin to put into practice the disciplinary actions of recognition and submission. These actions allow us to remove the overcoats and let the light so shine from inside that we begin according to the *law of attraction* to attract to us those like light forces that will emanate to us opportunities to expand in our awareness, our creation and to leave behind the painful decisions and experiences that we encounter while we sojourn in these valleys and climb these mountains.

As we begin this evolutionary process through time and space, we begin to recognize that on our sojourn on the earth plane there appears to be many different procedures, each one mystically guised in ritual. But underneath all that mystical ritual is simplicity and truth. No matter what ritual individuals are practicing, they are all going to eventually achieve the ultimate goal—evolution, and ascent through time and space through the understanding and application of these natural laws. They will look back at each recognition and say, "Yes, I was that all the time, but I failed to allow myself to see it. Now I am (being) it. As the karmic wheel spins with all of its dharma, I have the power, the strength and the understanding to bring about this pure light that emanates from within and allows me to move through my society being who I am." So we do know. It is only the intensification of these chosen karmic options that we encounter as we sojourn on the earth plane that make it appear like we don't know.

Seeker: I am afraid I will not adhere to all of these laws at all times. How do I deal with that?

Jordan: Are you dealing with your need to see yourself as Saint Rosi? Do you want everybody else to see you as Saint Rosi? Well, Rosi, I have news for you. You'd better open that book of yours. It's only your negative supporters who see you as the sacrificial Saint Rosi, who has gone through the trials and tribulations of the damned in her merciful mission of being here on the earth plane and descended in holy beauty, to smile upon these poor earthlings to give them healing. The best teacher is one who lives his life like an open book for everyone to see and says, "Here, read whatever you want to read. It's all here on the pages. I am working with it; you will be working with it."

There will be times that you know you are going to make judgments, but at least you will not complain when you have to pay the price. Don't worry, you're going to break the laws a thousand and one times, but you are in good company. I'll tell you now what a great teacher once said to me, "Did you expect me to be perfect? Did you expect yourself to be perfect? I am human; you are human. You will neither forget your human qualities nor your great spiritual qualities, and you will not forget my human qualities and my spiritual qualities." Then you start your process of real learning.

As long as you expect yourself to be perfect, you will constantly be hiding your imperfections and living a lie. If you expect me to be perfect, I'll show you repeatedly that I am not. Christ did the same thing. It's only the religious leaders who practice churchianity who want us to believe that Christ was absolutely perfect. But Christ showed us every aspect of himself because most of all he wanted humanity to know that they were his brothers and that the powers that he demonstrated they could demonstrate too.

All of your disciples will need to know that they can also demonstrate the powers that you demonstrate if they are willing to be as dedicated and as honest with themselves as you have been. Who would you rather be? Saint Rosi or a great teacher?

Seeker: If we adhere to the laws, we are all God in action?

Jordan: Of course, to the degree you allow it to manifest. Every thought, every action of a balanced, harmless nature that we enter into is God in action. It's got to have its effect on the atmosphere, the earth, on all those people who are receptive to it. Not only are we God in action, we are tracing the causes that have brought about the effects, and we are dealing with the compensations according to our understanding and submission to the effects. It's not hard to face the causes. The effect is you are in a physical body. You wouldn't be in a physical body if there wasn't a cause. You wouldn't be meeting each other, sharing opinions or expertises if there wasn't a cause. It is your job to be and to recognize who you are, not to be limited by the effect.

Seeker: Are some laws more powerful than others?

Jordan: When you are looking at the *laws of attraction, compensation* and *cause and effect*, you are looking at the three most powerful laws. They take away all of our excuses and justifications and force us to have to deal with ourselves instead of spending all of our time attempting to deal with other people and their reactions. This simple *law of attraction* causes us to get into some tremendous investigations about what attitudes, mind-sets and emotional limitations we were entering into that attracted us to our professions, our particular co-workers, and not only what we can learn about ourselves from them, but how we can activate our silent healing and teaching abilities.

In fact, all the laws are very important. But these three limit our negative projections, which act as destructive fodder for our planet, our atmosphere and our own spirit. When we really start working with these three laws, we will find ourselves more deeply in a place where we've got to deal with ourselves and activate techniques that will help us to change our conditions in our environments, not to wait for somebody else to do that for us. These three laws should be always activated together.

Our compensations should be very easily visible on the positive side as we encounter, on the highways of life, those illuminaries who plant the seeds of greater wisdom in our soil. They trust us to take gentle care of that seed, until it comes to fruition and becomes the young sapling that enjoys the sun's rays and the morning dew, and grows to a strong, sturdy tree that provides shelter and life for ever so many. It's the individuals that we meet on our pathway who see beyond our resistance, our self-judgments, our self-indulgences and say, "I love you regardless." They don't necessarily want to change us to fit their basic insecurities and needs, but they accept us carte blanche and are constantly on the giving end without extraction of commodities that would sustain them. Our good health is a wonderful compensation for activating these three laws and to the best of our abilities balancing them, seeing them in action in our life. That is part of our compensation.

In our financial environment, which once was overshadowed with anxiety and concern, we have come to that peaceful awareness that we need never be anxious or concerned again. For as long as we are functional, there will always be financial stability to allow us to move within society, continuing to drop our seeds of illumination, inspiration and encouragement.

There is the attraction and recognition of that soul companion we can unite with on whatever level is our choice. We derive tremendous support, inspiration, companionship from this union, even though we may be thousands of miles away from each other. The mere thought of them being active in our environment brings them close to us. Our children can be our positive compensations as we see ourselves reflected in them. We can take the steps, in a balanced way that our parents didn't, to break the cycle of reincarnated disruptions of vibration. We can lovingly say "This is what you can expect if you continue to function in this indulgence. Take a good look at me, because I learned from experience. Be my guest if that is what you want to do."

The positive effect of the *law of cause and effect* is that it stimulates our endeavors to get beyond the obvious. But many people get so caught up in the obvious compensations that they are reaping and identifying with from moment to moment that they never trace the cause of those intense malfunctions that affect them in their perceptions, attitudes and interpretations. Once we discover the cause of a condition, it leads us to accept that we've got the power to not get caught in the effect, but to do something to counteract and balance the cause, which then frees us to go on to another dimension of our self-recognition and growth. A surgical procedure, a magnetic healing, a divorce, a new job may relieve our discomfort but not catch our cause.

The *law of attraction,* when we recognize that we attracted it, allows us to give up being a victim, to stop seeing ourselves as an incapable, manipulable creature with no inner strength, constantly being manipulated by everything that we incurred in society, because we see ourselves as being punished and inferior to other people. There are few people who haven't felt manipulated, by a superior intelligence or a greater force, into things that they did not want to do. We all quake in our boots thinking about being subject to someone else's authority. Think of the positive results that can come when we can finally see that we are the creator of those attractions. The commodities that we have experienced in our environments we actually attracted. We created our parents to start the process of true parental forgiveness. What a freedom that is to be able to stand in our own shoes having truly forgiven that parental influence that we attracted and created as an active educational source in our environment. We can no longer be a victim of their tyranny, their cultural education, indoctrination, religious limitation. We've got to stand responsible for attracting it, because we chose it before we incarnated. We knew what we were going to be exposed to, and we had the ability to resist and to not identify with it. But think how much we have identified with it, how much we've let it influence every aspect of our life. That is a wonderful positive state of being to come from. So we can say now, "I'm going to do something about this."

There is a phrase: You can't cheat an honest man. An honest man will never know that he has been cheated, and nothing that we don't know exists. So we really can't cheat an honest man. We really can't hurt a loving man because his love will block the hurt. Attractions. I see it all as working in one direction of self-growth, self-recognition and redirection. Whatever we have attracted into our life, it is there as a learning opportunity.

Seeker: The laws are always in effect. So how do I apply something that is already in my life?

Jordan: It's applying your comprehension of it. The law is in effect, but many things are in effect. That doesn't mean that we recognize them, understand them, and it certainly doesn't guarantee that we live in accordance with them. That's our freedom of choice. We can choose what we want to live in accordance with. But if we look at our lives we can see in a physical, emotional and mental dimension what we have chosen to live in accordance with.

Seeker: Can each one of the Ten Commandments be traced back to natural law?

Jordan: Yes, each one of the Ten Commandments is definitely traceable to our comprehension of the natural laws as they pervade the universe, as they are in constant action within the universe.

Seeker: If we live by the natural laws, is it then important that we live by man's laws?

Jordan: Man's laws are a conglomerate of man's comprehension of the natural laws and how he applies them or refuses to apply them in his life. Even as we become spiritually evolved and aware of the dimensional existences that surround us, we still have to create a balance between our karmic/dharmic experiences in the physical and our karmic/dharmic awareness of what can be considered the unseen or the spiritual. We are in a position where we must constantly strive to achieve balance because balance is the keyword. Balance is necessary in our emotional, mental and physical bodies, which then allows us to express our spiritual perfection in a balanced way. Since we know the laws that govern karma and reincarnation, we realize that we are here to serve a purpose and to bring about an expression. As a result, we know that our next step is to bring about balance within ourselves.

So yes, we do have to abide, to a degree, by the societal inflicted laws that we have helped to formulate. I know that's hard to accept, but it isn't so hard when we start dealing with the idea of thoughts being things. When we recognize that our emotions are a great effective agent in the creation of the universes that we live with, then we can see more clearly as to how to apply the natural laws in man's conception of the laws in the society that we chose to be born or incarnated into. That then brings us to a place where we have to ask ourselves whether we are going to accept the concept of reincarnation and make it a part of our life. I believe that every seeker must come to that decision as he or she evolves in the evolutionary process.

Seeker: How do we deal with an unjust man's law?

Jordan: It wouldn't be in action if you hadn't helped to put it there. So it can't be unjust. There is nothing unjust, there is nothing undeserved. Who is the creator of your universe? (Seeker: I am.) If you truly believe that and accept that, then no one can create your universe unless you give him the power to do so. If you created a law that appears to be unjust, you should understand why you created it. You should use discernment instead of judgment and work constructively through your actions, not just your words, to ignite a greater awareness in the society that you chose to be incarnated into so that that "unjust" law can be altered. But you can't judge it, defy it and still be effective within the society that you have chosen and attracted to grow and evolve in.

Seeker: Which laws deal with emotional imbalance?

Jordan: The *laws of cause and effect, karma, "as above so below."* Emotional imbalance comes because we have encapsulated ourselves in a very tight little box that we find very comfortable and very secure. Even misery, poverty, ignorance can be very comfortable and give us a sense of security. Our physical identities and personalities are our sense of security. We really enjoy the mental exercise they give us; they make us feel as though we have life. Without it we wouldn't feel as though we have life. We like the stress that we place ourselves under. We like complaining about our physical ailments. We like to struggle financially. Believe it or not, we really enjoy it because it gives us something to talk about, to think about. If we didn't have that to think about, we definitely would have to think about our spiritual growth. We like to think about our lovers deserting us, whether we are even going to get a lover, because it gives us something to do with our brain. If we didn't have that to think about we might have to put our brain in a constructive mode and put our energies toward doing a good day's work— we might give our boss truly all the hours that he is paying us for. We like our family situations, our turmoil; it's comfortable for us. Going into the darkness of the unknown and putting all of our thought energies into what we are doing might make us successful, and what would we do if we were successful? So emotional imbalance comes from a totally inaccurate concept of ourselves.

Seeker: Is there a law of release?

Jordan: That is not a law, but it certainly is a constructive discipline that you have to enter into. You will find it very much in the *laws of cause and effect, compensation* and *attraction.* I believe that the action of releasing our old limitations and bringing in new thoughts is how we begin to use the laws more constructively. Release is actually a part of manifestation. You can't manifest anything until you release it and let it become strengthened.

        When we talk about the *law of attraction,* we say that like attracts like. When our thoughts are negative, unbalanced or balanced, they will attract like thoughts, like energies, which ultimately become an experience. So, if you are attempting to put into action the law of prosperity, you just simply can't go out and spend a lot of money and say, "Okay, now I have put all this money into working for me, now compensate me." You are going to be compensated by your thoughts and your emotions. That's why I always say that in order to manifest anything, you must lay down the old and accept the new. The action of actually spending money and proclaiming yourself as wealthy is similar to the action of doing yoga asanas. After the action, there must come some emotional and mental stability and belief, otherwise your action is absolutely empty. You can't just simply say "I am a psychic," if emotionally you don't feel like a psychic. You can't say "I release myself from my karma," when you still harbor judgment, anger and fear.

Seeker: Let's say I go down the list of the natural laws and concentrate on one law that attracts me the most—the *law of love.* I do everything to abide by this law. If I manage to do that, I would automatically abide by all the other laws. That would mean that every law is automatically contained within all the other laws. Is that correct?

Jordan: No, they are not. I wish I could tell you that they are, but they are not. But it takes about three minutes, just before you fall asleep, to affirm, in a positive statement, that you love every part of you. That is putting the *law of love* into action. In the *law of cause and effect,* if you keep a dream journal and a motivation journal, it's going to lead you to an understanding of where you are either in harmony or out of harmony with the *law of cause and effect.* Then you can start pragmatically to change what you don't like. Those are steps that don't take a lot of time.

With the *law of compensation* you can take a look at your family situation, your emotional situation and apply the *law of non-judgment* and practice discernment. Look at the situation realistically. You already know that you created it. Ask yourself what you want to change. Then start working on yourself. Don't direct your efforts to your mate, your boss, your parents. Direct them to yourselves. Let the natural laws work for you. There is nothing wrong with you discerning what you created thus far. There is something wrong if you surrender to it, if you let yourself be victimized. That's not being in harmony with the laws. You can work on them all at one time. But don't try to evaluate how quickly they are put into action. You've got nothing but time; use it in a balanced, understanding, directed way. All of that will come into harmony. The *law of compensation* will work for you. You will create situations that will support your new self-awareness.

If you've dealt with a sense of inferiority and you start projecting a sense of equality, the *law of compensation* is going to prove to you that you are worthy. You are going to start seeing your effectiveness with more of humanity. People are going to come and gravitate towards you, they will want to hear you, see you, be with you. You are going to enjoy the knowledge you'll get from associating with people because they will show you where you just came from. It's going to help you in every measure of your life.

So don't try to center on just one law because then you are going to sit there and concentrate on it. "Are you working? Where are you? Are you there somewhere? I heard you exist." Don't make that mistake.

Natural laws and success

Seeker: In adhering to the natural laws, would you please talk about the necessity of being disciplined in order to become successful?

Jordan: You can't look at success and say, "I am beating at your door, but I really don't want you," because success then says, "Fine, then I'll go to someone else." If you want a successful center, start living like you have a successful center. If you want to be spiritual, don't be just part-time spiritual. You are spiritual 24 hours a day and you apply spirituality to your work, and all of a sudden there is a little turn of a switch. If you want a beautiful body, you discipline it. If you want a beautiful face, you stand there and put all the cosmetics on. All is discipline. It begins with discipline, with self-realization, and it brings you to success: *law of compensation, law of attraction* and *law of cause and effect.* Hopefully you will choose things that are harmless to you, and you will have applied the *law of harmlessness.* Because if you are harmful to yourself, you are also being harmful to your brothers and sisters.

As you discipline, recognize, accept and understand yourself, you are also applying the *law of love.* When you are loving yourself, you can love me. If you can't love yourself because you have broken the *law of non-judgment* and the *law of non-comparison,* then unfortunately, you must start by disciplining yourself to love me and to apply the *law of obedience.* It is only through obedience and submission that you gain everything. I have taught all of you to be cautious, to look wisely and carefully, and to make sure that you are not with someone who wants to own you, control you and use you. You know that I don't want to own you, control you or use you. As a result, submission and obedience should be easy, because, ultimately, you are submitting to the good in yourself, which you see in me, and you are being obedient to the wisdom that you hear in me that's in you. But you have never recognized or accepted the *law of like attracts like.* As a result you all want to feel different; you all want to foster your karma instead of entertaining your dharma. I am waiting for you to entertain your dharma.

You are not even entertaining logic. If you would apply one tenth of what I teach you, you wouldn't have business problems, marriage problems, health problems because you would heal and cure them. Why are you so stressed? I have taught you colorology, the laws, the power of verbalization. I have taught you the necessity to regenerate your cell bodies through meditation. I taught you how to be obedient to all of the energies in the atmosphere. I taught you that you are a sponge. I've told you how you can project your aura. You are dealing with problems because you won't deal with the *law of cause and effect.* You won't look at the effects in your life and say, "That's in my life because I have created it, and I have created it out of my insecurity, my inadequacy. I broke the *laws of non-comparison, non-judgment* and *non-force,* and I wouldn't believe in the *law of divine order.* That's why I have this problem." Do you know when you are released from the karma of your own personality? When it no longer affects or manipulates you. You are never released from any karma until you control it.

Everybody wants a free ticket to heaven, but heaven is a state of consciousness. Love is something you nurture and grow, and success is something you nurture and grow. It is not something that is automatically thrown at you. Don't look to other people for recognition. If you don't recognize yourself, how will they? Are you ready to commit yourself? Are you ready

to change the frequencies that you have been laboring under all these years? Or will it take more pain? A
teacher must sit back and watch his students create
all the pain for themselves and know, beyond a shadow
of a doubt, they don't need it, so they must want it.
And, if they want it, God bless them. Let them have
it, because it's something that's good for them. If you
tell a child not to put his hand in the fire, and he
does, from the burn he recognizes the *law of cause and
effect.*

Seeker: What do I need to do in my meditation in order to
get everything I want?

Jordan: Start working on your insight. Stop doubting. What
keeps the *law of attraction* from fulfilling itself? Your
own self-doubt. There is a little statement that absolutely encompasses everything. When something
doesn't manifest, it's because you didn't believe it
would, you didn't want it badly enough. So that's a
good learning lesson. You attracted non-manifestation
to you. It tells you that you have to find out where
you didn't manifest. May be you were totally undisciplined and unschooled, and you didn't believe in yourself. You were scared to death to jump in the water
and swim, to deal with your own self. It is much easier
to be a failure and to blame everybody else than it is
to be a success and have to administrate success. But,
you are going to get it, because there is that small
voice inside of you that says, "I am going to get the
answers to my questions, and I am not afraid of exposing myself." As a result you are three steps ahead,
because most people think, "What will the others
think of me?" Thus, they never get the answers to
their questions. It is a fool for a minute who asks the
questions, but is a fool for eternity who asks no questions.

Seeker: The thoughts I put out in the astral realm are rein-
forced by other thoughts?

Jordan: Yes, by thoughts of a like nature. When you are actually practicing prosperity, you try to associate with prosperity. When you are actually practicing the *law of love,* you try to associate with persons who express it. You discipline yourself and choose not to allow yourself to be influenced by absorbing vibratory energies that are less than those you want to attract. It would be silly to do that because you would bring your own self down. You would create your own self-destruction and your own self-limitation. You have to think prosperously, feel prosperously and act prosperously in order to get prosperity. And you have to give prosperously in order to put the law into action. You can't just say it with your mouth, you have to think it and feel it. You can't apply the laws just with your mouth. I hear that many of you obey the laws with the mouth, but your emotions tell me a different story. You put all those emotional energies out into the atmosphere, and when they come back as living experiences you wonder and question why things didn't work out for you. It's because you said it only with your mouth.

Seeker: We look at ourselves, we come to a point where we find ourselves feeling more secure in certain self-understandings. We believe that it is not just an intellectualization. And then, something happens and we feel like we are starting all over again.

Jordan: You have no one else to believe in except you. If you will recognize the *law of attraction,* you will actually realize that like attracts like on the many dimensional and frequency levels. You are attracting to you exactly what you are requesting for your own testing.

Read the book of Job. You don't conquer Job simply because you put emotional or physical stops on your behavior. You have to have intellectual understanding and emotional discipline. Emotional discipline comes through faith, obedience and acceptance. You have no one to accept but yourself. When you work on yourself, then you will automatically attract to you more influential beings.

Acceptance. I am what I am, and what I am needs no excuses. What you are needs no excuses. If you like it, you are entitled to wear it. If you don't like it, you are entitled to discipline it. That's what you refuse to do. You keep bombarding the lower astral plane with all the thoughts of limitation, and you think you are doing yourself a justice by using mouth service. That doesn't cut it. You have four bodies. Three of which, the emotional, mental and physical must all be in unity. The fourth body, the spiritual body, is always perfect. So whatever action you take you have to be disciplined in it. The *law of cause and effect* says, that from the lower astral plane, you are going to attract like energies into your physical being. It is up to you to believe you are wealthy. It is up to you to do the disciplines to express that you are wealthy and to act wealthy. If you are dealing with poverty, confusion, doubt, anxiety, disruption in your goal, ask yourself why you have attracted these things to you. You attract them to you as excuses because of your fears of the responsibility of obtaining your goals. With every karmic evolution we acquire in our journey on this earth plane, it brings about responsibility and the necessity to make choices and to discipline ourselves. Having wealth, beauty, a glib tongue, being a wonderful spiritual being or a fabulous musician—all have their responsibilities. You have to be prepared to accept success. You have to be flexible; you have to be willing to let go of the old in order to get the new.

Gender and the laws

Seeker: You said that many women have a female body but are actually men. Does the soul have a gender, and what is the purpose of a gender?

Jordan: The soul has no gender. The soul is a perfect composite of the yin and the yang. The soul is supposed to be a composite of the masculine and the feminine, projecting a balanced energy into the atmosphere so that the *law of compensation* can manifest itself in the physical dimension, the *law of cause and effect* can come into action in the unseen dimensions. The *law of divine order* brings us to a place where we can see beyond the limitations of the eyes and the cell bodies that normally are in action to create our physical and emotional dimensions of life. I would equate the *law of cause and effect* with lower astral life; I would equate the *law of divine order* with upper astral projection or upper astral life, which is what you come into contact with when you are in a dream state. The soul is asexual. It can be either masculine or feminine according to the *laws of cause and effect* and *compensation.* And it deals with the *law of divine order.* The soul actually emanates the energy from divine order. We have a difficult time in comprehending and accepting this because each of us enters into creative, constructive actions without really recognizing the *law of compensation* in action, and we create from an illusionary concept of our physical identity.

We have chosen masculine or feminine forms. We have chosen them because they give us the greatest opportunity to be able to bring a balance from this unseen emotionally felt world. That's why I relate it back to the psychologist, the psychiatrist, the waitress, the salesman, etc., who work a great deal from gut reaction, which they cannot, in the *law of compensation,* relate to. The *law of compensation* represents the physical ailments and limitations that we inflict upon ourselves in their densest commodity. When we are dealing with spinal column problems, with meridians and muscles that are over-tense, the body is saying that we have, for one purpose or another, stayed too long in a particular frequency and have absorbed the imbalances of those individuals in our association. Compensation tells us what we are doing.

Suppose you are a counselor, a teacher, a psychologist, a salesman and you measure your worth, your identity by how many jobs you get or how many products you sell. You are already entering into a malfunction. You should be out there in action with the realization that people will buy what they think they need. You don't have to overextend yourself in order to create your solvency. We do the same thing with the vibration of love. We send out, from an emotional factor, the idea that we must lose our whole identity in order to be able to gain love, because in the *law of compensation* we are experiencing our own reluctance to understand and accept ourselves and to know that we have the power to discipline ourselves. In turn this means that we must overextend ourselves in the expression of love to prove to other individuals that we love them, which brings about a physical, emotional and intellectual reaction. This reaction was stirred by our own mental lack of comprehension of ourselves. So we have created physical, emotional and mental destruction that says, "Stop, look and listen." That's the *law of compensation* in action.

Vortex between compensation and cause and effect

Seeker: Do we have to create a vortex between the *laws of compensation* and *cause and effect?*

Jordan: You have to create the vortex between each of these laws in order to be able to understand. Through many of your disciplines (dietary, philosophical, etc.) in the *law of compensation* you have begun to use control measures on your thoughts, actions and words. You have altered and changed the light and done a little chipping away at some of the dross that surrounds your philosopher's stone inside of your own being, and the light shines through you. So you begin, through the *law of compensation,* to attract an ease from the disease that caused you to begin to search.

That's why I use Edgar Cayce and Fletcher as examples because Edgar Cayce lived his life telling people where they had created the karmic and dharmic illusion of their life, how to conquer it and what attitudes to approach in order to be able to conquer the illusion. That brought them with a vortex into the *law of cause and effect*. If I tell you the physical *law of compensation* governs the lower astral plane, where all of your embryos and all of your thoughts that you think nobody is aware of gather moss and eventually become effective in your life, then it should be common sense that as you become master of the *law of compensation*, you then become master of cause and effect. Many times people have called me and said, "I really want to come and study with you, but I don't have the money. My heart tells me I should be there every time you are teaching, but I don't come because money is a problem." They are out of conjunction with the *law of compensation*. They are like drug pushers who are out there on the street pushing drugs. They justify all their reasons for doing so because they think it will open the portal to the *law of cause and effect*. What are they doing when the God of them is telling them and emanating that they are totally out of balance and they will ultimately pay the price for it? What are they doing with it? They are putting more imbalance into the *law of cause and effect*.

Karma and the law of "as above so below"

Seeker: Please say more about karma and the *law of "as above so below."*

Jordan: Everything that you are at this point in time is the assimilation of the karmas that you have agreed to fulfill in this lifetime. The *law of "as above so below"* is indicative of all those loose, disjointed and unbalanced thoughts that you project into the lower astral planes. They will be there, acting as a magnet, attracting according to the *law of attraction* like thoughts of the same dimensions and degrees until they become solidified experiences. These experiences then produce physical, mental and emotional illness and problematic situations in your daily life.

According to my knowledge of karma and what you have agreed to fulfill, in order to reach through and enter a greater dimension of understanding, you have to begin to balance your karma so that you can enter those greater dimensions. That's why you are all studying philosophy. You are all attempting, in your own degrees and ways, to put this understanding into action in your lives. You want to move through the cycles of karmic flow, but your physical bodies don't assimilate wisdom from just one past lifetime. It comes from an embodiment of all lifetimes. You move through attitudes, concepts, understandings, which can be attributed to other lifetimes.

For example, if you find cooking easy and you become an expert at it, you can be assured that you were an expert cook in another lifetime and you are bringing back that knowledge.

If you sit down at a keyboard and all of a sudden you start playing with a genius quality, you can be assured that you have been a genius musician in a past lifetime. The dharma is how you use a gift when you discover it.

If you start working with metaphysics and you get turned on to philosophy and all of a sudden it becomes second nature to you, you can be assured that in many past lifetimes you used metaphysics as a tool and became an expert at it.

There is nothing new under the heaven or on the earth. All things that are, have been. So you actually have assimilated the atom structure that allows you to fulfill your karmic responsibilities, to bring about your dharmic influences. And, whether you know it or not, the choices that you make bring about, either karmically or dharmically, the experiences that you need or desire to encounter. But your choice is there. And all of your thoughts enter into the astral planes where they gather strength. There they are affected and influenced by everyone else's thoughts of a like nature because, you must remember, the *law of like attracts like.*

Desires, natural laws and our spirit guides

Jordan: All of our desires are usually based in conjunction with the *law of cause and effect.* We recognize the cause. The cause is either the balance or the imbalance of our interpretation of ourselves and the energy pattern that we experience exteriorly. It is either the balanced or the unbalanced interpretation of hopes and dreams that are sometimes an awareness of a past life accomplishment or a past life association. We want to experience some of it again in this particular life's expression, and so we start looking at the *law of cause and effect.* We recognize that our desires emanate from an existing cause, and we try to find the cause. Ultimately, as we work with the *law of compensation* in our life, we know we have just about everything that we are entitled to have. We are compensated for those physical happenings, emotional upheavals and mental stimuli according to the actions and expressions that we have entered into. We are offered options and opportunities for expansion on a regular basis according to our self-recognition, our self-understanding and our self-directions.

When we are working with cause and effect, and desire to work much more completely with our spiritual forces, we must deal with the *law of compensation* and recognize that our spirit guides that we know exist around about us in this lifetime are our compensation from past life endeavors. They are already there. As we are working with cause and effect and desire, we have to determine what is motivating the desire. What aspect of our duality are we attempting to pacify, to indulge?

After all, we can't expect our spirit guides to indulge our personality. But so many of us desire to have our physical and our emotional personality needs met.

So we start projecting our desires and wishes out into the universe, demanding that they manifest. And we expect our guides and teachers to manifest them for us. But our guides and teachers aren't going to manifest anything for us that we don't believe we are worthy of or entitled to. They continue to show it to us, we continue to desire it, but we only get portions of it or a bit of it because we don't really believe we are worthy of it.

Seeker: I want my Indian (one of the spirit guides) to bring me into closer contact with the nature spirits, so that my personality does not interfere in my communication with my patients and I can communicate in a balanced way.

Jordan: Start out with the *law of divine order.* If someone is dealing with schizophrenia or AIDS, or any malfunction, that's divine order for them. That's your patient's learning lesson. He is not a victim, he is the creator of it. Your job is to channel the balance that will give him choice factors and help him to cure himself. But don't you believe that you are doing the curing, because, as a doctor, you should know you can't cure anyone unless he or she wants to be cured. That's how you keep your personality out of it. You keep your Indian active by knowing everything is in divine order. Your job is to be able to communicate with nature and see yourself as just another part of nature, communicating in a balanced way.

Being a custodian for God and the laws

Seeker: Would you talk about being the custodian for God?

Jordan: God has given us everything, and we as the custodians use it for the evolvement and advancement of ourselves and others. If you want something, you don't have to save for it. All you have to do is know that you are worthy of it. You have to clear up your obstacles—emotionally, mentally, physically. You have to apply the *law of obedience,* you have to put into action what you have learned. It is called God in action. You have to put Him into action in every facet of your life. When you start doing things for God, you no longer do them for yourself. When you do something for God, you get the best in return.

Now don't get me wrong. I am not saying, "Don't save," not at all. I am saying it is your attitude that is delaying what you are saving for, because your saving is merely a discipline, just like vegetarianism, which proves you to yourself. Once you have saved the amount you want, then you feel that you are worthy of the object. Why not be worthy of the object before you have saved the amount, knowing the money will come to you. That's putting the *law of compensation* into action. As you give of your belief, faith, trust and obedience, the object of your desire will come to you. It's up to you to put the law into action. If you compare and measure yourself as being inadequate, then you must enter into a discipline to become adequate. If you ignore your emotional, mental and physical imbalance when it is telling you a story, it becomes a fact, and then you have to accept the story. When you begin to release, when you begin to feel that through your discipline, motivation and direction, you have finally made yourself worthy of the object, then you buy it, then you accept it. You want it? Go for it and pay the price for it.

We don't have to like the way of life today. But, if we choose to love it, and when we actually put the law into action, where then is the abundance really coming from? Does it come from our labors, from our minor, meager intellect, or does it come from a source that's greater than us? In reality it comes from a greater source. The *law of attraction* tells us: The more we attune to the source, the more abundance we get. The more we clear up the obstacles in our life, the more peace we get. The more we don't recognize our fears and don't discipline them, the more we will experience the manifestation of our fears in the physical. The more we believe that people don't understand us, don't like us, the more we cause them to be exactly that way with us. That's the *law of attraction*. If we believed and projected acceptance and understanding because we are giving it to ourselves, we would get it from other people, because they've got to respond to the *law of attraction*. We pay for every action, every thought, every emotional emanation. That's why the *law of "as above so below"* is in action. If we discipline ourselves, if we put forth our best effort, then we know, whether it is today, tomorrow or the next day, it is going to come back to us.

You try to apply the law while you are holding on to the strings. That indicates a lack of faith. You apply lip service. There is no reason for you not to trust yourself, not to have faith in yourself. If you need more schooling, go and get it. If you put the thought out, you attract it to you if you believe and are ready to work with it. Many of you have asked me, "Why don't I have the perfect companion?" and I have asked you, "What would you give him?" and you answer, "Very little." So, how can you get your perfect companion if you want to subject him to your imbalance?

Seeker: When I realize that I've made a lot of mistakes and have had a lot of bad thoughts, do I have to stop thinking those thoughts?

Jordan: Your question should be how to stop those thoughts. You do it by accepting them, without judgment, without comparison, and by beginning to discipline them. I am what I am, and what I am needs no excuses, because what I am grows. You become static and steeped in karma when you refuse to accept what you are. Only when you cease to judge and compare yourself can you be yourself. Pull in all those antennas that are directed out to interpret the expectation, the visualization and the awareness of how you think others are evaluating you, and come to your own evaluation. Look at your life. Is it perfect? If it was, you wouldn't be here. You are looking for something, and you hope to find it here. Don't compare yourself, just accept that all these people are looking for the same thing. Pull in your antenna and let it show you yourself. That's the only way you can accept what you are. Simply say, "I am what I am, and that's no limitation. And I will be better and greater tomorrow." That's how you do it.

You don't wash your "lions" out of the body. You can't really wash cancer or diabetes out of your body until you stop the cause. You've got to accept the cause and discipline yourself. You say, "This is the cause, but it doesn't need to control me." No one else can do it for you. No one can make you feel good about yourself, except temporarily.

Seeker: Do we need a teacher to comprehend these natural laws?

Jordan: The visions you hold of yourselves are your destructive commodities, because you are holding onto man's law and won't bridge the gap and understand natural law. That's why you need a teacher who makes demands on you because he knows you are. Anything that prohibits you from being all that you are is buying into man's law.

A student starts a journal and then, when the student is ready, he finds a teacher. What if I tell you I think you are one of the most beautiful and most talented persons I know? You are going to say that's nonsense. It's what you say to yourself that is your lesson to learn. That is what you begin to work on. That's why we seek and find a teacher, a therapist, etc., because we want to experience what he or she sees in us and not what we see about ourselves.

Student/Teacher Dialogues

Why do I have to subject myself to these laws?

Seeker: God is almighty and unlimited. I am God in my own universe. So why do I have to subject myself to these laws?

Jordan: Because you created them and you must live under your creations.

Seeker: They are irreversible?

Jordan: No, once you live under and with your creations and you understand why you created them and you internalize them, they no longer exist externally.

These laws are God in action

Seeker: These laws seem to have intelligence and awareness. Who determines the natural laws?

Jordan: First of all, the laws' intelligence exists because it represents balanced energy, undefined energy.

Seeker: Could one say God is behind these laws?

Jordan: We can say all of these laws are God in action. But we interpret them. We set up the punishment that brings these laws back into balance by our recognition as to when we are out of balance, out of harmony with the energy patterns, the life force in the universe. When we start attempting to run in the opposite direction of the life force, we create a frictional action. When two opposites come together, they don't merge. They create a frictional reaction, and that frictional reaction is the law in action.

Seeker: What about grace? Christ gave me absolution, and that is not explainable by those laws.

Jordan: Oh yes, it is. It's the *law of love*. It is through our Christ consciousness that we unconditionally love our existing conditions, circumstances, states of understanding and get the information from them. The information then sets us free. But Christ's whole purpose was to come and physically demonstrate the results of living in harmony, in rhythm with the God force, of seeing no other power with more authority than the power of his Father. He loved Pilate, he loved his crucifiers, he loved the leper, he loved the blind; he didn't see them as second-class citizens, as permanently afflicted beings. He went right to the core of their imbalance and he healed their imbalance, not just their disorder. He instructed them: Now that you are in harmony, now that you have been healed, go and sin no more.

Similarity of laws

Seeker: It seems that the *laws of compensation, cause and effect* and *attraction* are pretty much the same.

Jordan: No, they are very different. You can get compensation not only from past lives, but you can certainly get instantaneous compensation. For a cause to bring about an effect, it takes a great deal of continued indulgence in the action before the effect becomes so prevalent in your environment that you can't deny it. So there is a big difference. You can have a compensation in action that you are dealing with on a day-to-day basis. But having reincarnated into this country known as Germany, that compensation in action is not going to bring you into an awareness of the cause that brought about the effect until you investigate and accept for yourself the premise or the thesis of reincarnation and rebirth. You can have some compensations that are related to your female suit that you are wearing that may not necessarily expose the cause.

Seeker: So the *law of cause and effect* refers primarily to past lives and reincarnation?

Jordan: It refers to a lengthy indulgence in an attitude or an encapsulation, which has brought about an undeniable effect in your physical, mental and emotional makeup.

Seeker: But in both, *compensation* and *cause and effect,* the *law of attraction* is functioning because we are always attracting the same energies.

Jordan: On the contrary. When you alter and expand in your consciousness you begin to attract—but not necessarily experience—extensions, expansions, and assistances which can provide opportunities to enable you to step beyond your normal levels of attraction. You can start working on a physical discipline and make this body a replica of Arnold Schwarzenegger or Elizabeth Taylor, and you will be compensated for that action. You may not necessarily understand the *law of cause and effect,* but you will be compensated for that effort. You may not necessarily understand all of the attractions that brought about the action of adhering to a discipline that produced a replica of the Arnold Schwarzenegger form or of the Elizabeth Taylor form, etc.

Chain of command amongst the laws

Seeker: Is there a chain of command in these laws?

Jordan: I would always look first at the *law of attraction.* I would work with it and accept the fact that I have attracted into my political, social, economic, philosophical, emotional, intellectual and physical environments all of those energies that will help me to see my compensations for indulged-in self-judgment, self-comparison, self-criticism or encapsulation that doesn't necessarily lead me to this *law of cause and effect* that asks why. With the *law of attraction* you can ask: What are you doing here? With the *law of compensation* you can ask: What are you telling me? But then you've got to get to the *law of cause and effect* to discover its total purpose for being there. Too many of us on superficial levels can accept compensation in action. The question usually asked is: "Why did they do that to me?" So he is recognizing that there is a compensation in action. He doesn't understand how it all manifested. When you encounter disruptive situations that affect your plans for yourself look at your own questions. You will ask "Why did they do that to me?" "Why didn't the plane fly?" "Why didn't the business bring in the money it should have?" Only after greater clarity will you come to terms with the *law of attraction,* and that you attracted it to yourself.

The laws are not at all similar. You can be careless in your kitchen and cut off your finger, and you will get the compensation for your carelessness. But that doesn't mean you had to cut off your finger because of the *law of cause and effect.*

Seeker: Carelessness would be the cause, wouldn't it?

Jordan: No, carelessness would be the indulgence and the compensation would be the loss of your finger.

Falsity in spirituality and the laws

Seeker: Please describe what falseness in spirituality is.

Jordan: Untruth. Lack of commitment. Do your spiritual forces give you wrong information? Don't you get everything that they say you are going to get? Is it delayed? If it's delayed, you'd better look at the *laws of divine order, cause and effect* and *compensation.* That's what the *law of like attracts like* means. No one controls that but you. If I tell you that you are the master and captain of all the laws, that should tell you that you must learn to control the laws.

You can find many people who are going to tell you how great and wonderful you are. But, unfortunately you will never find anybody who tells you how stupid you are and does it lovingly. I will, because I don't mind your negative projections. When you beat yourselves, it's only another escape into the *law of compensation.* I don't beat you, you beat yourselves. I just tell you what you need to work on. Accept it, deal with it, and go from there.

Other planetary forces and the law of attraction

Seeker: People who feel attacked by outer space beings, is that a reality?

Jordan: It's a reality. What makes us believe that this is the only planet with a life force? How foolish can we really be to think that?

Seeker: I am just thinking of somebody who feels attacked—

Jordan: They are not dealing with their own interior violence. They are not dealing with their own interior desire for self-destruction. You must recognize the *law of like attracts like,* and it doesn't necessarily have to come from this planetary dimension. Our astral body is not governed by the *law of gravity.* Gravity is an effect to keep our pollution in this space so it doesn't get out there and pollute the other dimensions. But our astral body can move anywhere, because it is only energy and is not governed by the *law of gravity.* So if we are projecting self-destruction, there are lots of forces out there that are going to do it for us.

How do you know that a great part of you, while you are sitting here attached to the shell you call your body, is not on the planet Mercury creating disruption there?

Seeker: Which part would that be?

Jordan: It could be those unconscious, unrecognized and denied thoughts that are going somewhere, some place.
How do you know that what you are doing now in
your unrecognized attitudes and indulgences isn't creating the scenarios you are going to live with five years
from now?

How to introduce the concept of reincarnation

Seeker: How do you introduce the idea of reincarnation to a
person?

Jordan: I've spent 25 years struggling to learn how to introduce the idea of reincarnation, in counseling or in
any kind of work, in an attempt to bring about an
awareness of an existing cause, which brings about an
existing effect. I have never absolutely found the most
balanced way of doing it. People expect theoretical
concepts from me anyway, so they just listen to it as a
theoretical concept and go back and do it their way.

But I always try to feel out the situation. I might
refer to an energy influence that is prevalent around
about them. Oftentimes they put their own label on
it. I don't think there is any balanced way to introduce the potential, unless you use genealogy as an
entrance to the *law of cause and effect*. Because science
and medicine support the concept of genealogy, so
you can go from there. But the minute you tell someone or try to inform someone, that they have brought
with them a tendency from when they were a soldier
in Rome and killed everybody, you've got a problem.
And it is a major one.

Seeker: Can you give me an example involving genealogy?

Jordan: You can say, someone is governing their creative ability by the limitations that they have absorbed and
taken onto themselves through heritage and genealogy. Of course, when we speak about heritage, we are
speaking of religious and philosophical concepts of
behavior patterns that individuals enter into because

of expectations. We talk about the labelization they do to themselves, such as, I'm a Catholic, I'm a Protestant, I'm a Jew, etc., etc. You can touch into the concept of reincarnation by referring to that particular statement. Then you can go on to say, "Look at the characteristics of your parents to see, through genealogy, what you personally are going to be influenced by. That does not mean controlled by, it means influenced by. You have the choice to break that pattern." Those are the only methods I have ever been able to use.

Compensation, cause and effect and divine order

Seeker: If cause and effect is a gut reaction, what then is divine order?

Jordan: Divine order is spiritual insight. It is only when you apply divine order that you can move into that totally balanced frequency. Divine order says that everything is balanced. You only get life when you recognize divine order in action. There is no balance as long as you're dealing with personality influence, which shows that you're not into clairvoyance. Clairvoyance sees that everything that affects is for a purpose. As a psychic, you cannot afford to make judgments, coagulations, encapsulations and determinations. You must be an open vehicle that says everything is in divine order. There is no right, there is no wrong, it just is, and it's going to bring a fulfillment of either karma and dharma, or it's going to be a compensation for the thought and word emanations that people are expressing in the physical dimension. Because by our spoken word and by our thought patterns are we known. That's why in the scriptures it's said, "By their works they shall be known." Works were more important than words because there were a lot of the wise men who spoke a good case, but didn't live a good case. There were also a lot of Egyptians who spoke wisely as priests and priestesses, and lived as harlots in the temples of the living God of Egypt and Tibet.

We constantly get compensation in every facet of our life. We divide our life into four parts—mental, emotional, physical and spiritual, and we find compensation from all of them. But ultimately, we are attempting to leave behind not the *law of compensation* but the influences of the *law of compensation* on a day-to-day basis. This encourages us to begin to pursue our spiritual life and to move into the *law of cause and effect*. It's only when we have moved into the *law of cause and effect* that we can apply the understanding, knowledge and wisdom that brought about our entrance into the *law of cause and effect* and allows us to begin to assume some of the responsibilities and obligations from our past life associations. This then begins to break the chains that bind us and make it necessary for us to return to physical density.

Mostly, what we experience in the physical life plane expression with our identities of "John Doe" is the *law of compensation*. We are compensated by our thoughts, words and actions. That's why we have such institutes as Silva Mind Control, Transcendental Meditation, etc., because they deal with moment-to-moment thinking. They cause us to put restraint on our emotions and our thinking so that we can begin to create a vortex that causes us to move into the cause and effect dimension of the natural laws. We then associate with individuals who we've had and have a karmic or a dharmic indebtedness with.

Seeker: Would the association be both dharmic and karmic with each individual?

Jordan: No, not necessarily. Ultimately you should learn to apply the *law of compensation,* and you should learn the mental and emotional attitudes and the physical dexterity and disciplines that allow you to create a vortex to enter into the frequency level of the *law of cause and effect*. During your sojourn on the earth plane, if you meet a karmic association that brings about what appears to be pain, depravity, anxiety or whatever the case may be, then the only way to turn it into a dharmic understanding is by applying the *law of divine order.* That means that you neither judge it nor do you encapsulate it, nor do you attempt to intellectualize it. But you know it's an opportunity for you to put forth the very best of what you have learned in the frequency that is governed by the *law of compensation.* That's how we turn karma into dharma, through our comprehension of it and our working through it. We cannot abort it; we cannot escape the many cycles through which our karma and dharma express once we have earned entrance into the cause and effect frequency. We can't escape it; we must work through it. As we do, it becomes less and less effective in our life.

For example, I know that I am a hopeless flirt, and I know that I flirt because my karma is to be insecure about my own personal status. If I discipline that, understand that, know it, work with it, then it becomes my dharma. But if I become engrossed and incorporated in it then it becomes my karma, because it controls me rather than me controlling it.

Seeker: In other words, you can utilize it to bring about growth in individuals instead of feeling that you need the strokes?

Jordan: Exactly. All of the attributes that you're given, once you understand why you've been given them, can be used to bring about the greatest degree of growth in individual bodies. It is entirely up to you as to how you use it. But the *law of compensation* shows you when you've been using it erroneously. You just have to take responsibility for your own life. Unfortunately, we like to pass our life on to everybody else. But then we have talked many times about the Pilates of our lives, and how we give them total power over us as opposed to using them to our best advantage.

Seeker: When we have emotionally detached and we are able to make a clear intellectual evaluation, it feels often-times very cold. How can we merge with the spiritual?

Jordan: By implementing the *law of divine order*. As we detach from the emotional influence in our evaluation of any of the active situations we create in our life, and work strictly from intellect, we can bridge the gap between educated intellect and God intellect by applying divine order.

Karma and the laws

Seeker: Suppose I have a karmic obligation. The law of karma demands today that I experience—

Jordan: The law of karma demands that you understand that experience and recognize its effect in your life, upon your life, and that you learn the lessons from it. It either requires actual in-battle experience, or you learn through osmosis. That is your choice. But you are going to experience it one way or the other, the hard way or the easy way. All through life, everyone of us, day by day, moment by moment, faces that choice and faces our fears. We can either choose to learn our lessons the easy way or the hard way. The hard way is in war, in battle with the fears, the anxieties and all the aftermath that comes from the indulgence of those fears and anxieties. Or we can choose to learn it the easy way.

For example: You are sitting in this class right here and now, so you've made a choice in evolvement. Let's say the subject matter is coping with our fears. Since our fears are the basic cause that brings about the effects of an unbalanced nature, which we are fighting with on a day-to-day basis, you can choose to either learn about your fears through osmosis by recognizing them and choosing to put into practice the disciplines that will allow you to understand: why the fear, how to cope with it, how to work with it, and how to use it in a constructive manner. Or you can choose to ignore your fears, cover over your fears, and continue to emanate their energy into the atmospheric conditions, which will then bring the experience into effect. Then you must live with the experience until you have understood why the experience is there.

When you are faced with karmic situations that have family ties, emotional ties, friendship ties, occupational ties, religious ties, you're going to be in battle with them until such time as you can understand their value, their purpose, their lesson, and you incorporate it in the expansion of your imagery, your self-imagery, and you actually begin to flow in your self-imagery.

Those are your two choices in the physical dimension. But the ultimate end result is that you are going to live and you are going to evolve.

Death from pain in this dimension? Unfortunately, many of our spirit friends find, when they cross over the line, that they encounter monumental pain of a different nature. They see all of the choices they made and actions they took while in physical bodies, while governed by physical personalities that were governed by fears. They see the mistakes, as you would call them, that they made. Then they must choose if they will work through the results of these choices and actions on the lower astral plane, which, if there is a measurement, can take eons of centuries. Or they must be confronted with their choices and actions in the physical and in the personality and work through it. These are the things you are going to do, and it doesn't matter how any of you try to avoid it. You can avoid it for this lifetime, that is your choice; you can avoid facing your fears in this lifetime. But because of your creative measure, you will compound them. The more you compound them, the more you will tip the scales. And as you tip the scales, you then have to, through your works and through your understanding, balance out the scales until you can walk through life in balance. You are going to be confronted by your anxieties, your trepidation, your fears—by absolutely everything that you can possibly experience in life, in the physical dimension. Those experiences do not alter and do not change when you leave this personality, this assimilation of densified atom structure.

There is this *law of "as above so below."* This is one of our hope factors. Above in the higher astral plane, we get the vision of our true identity, our true purposes, such as being a healer, a teacher, a medium. We start, by the *law of attraction,* to bring that higher astral plane energy through the atmospheric dimensions and we begin to drink it in through our cell tissues. We then begin to mirror it, to reflect it into the physical dimensions. That's an assistance to us, a benefit. But we will also encounter that creation in the lower dimension where all of our fears, anxieties and confusions are. If we indulge in our fear process, our doubt process, our incomplete vision process, then we zoom out with our magnetic energy right to the lower dimensions, and we open the portal for all of that intensified energy to be drawn right into our beings. It increases our fears, our trepidation, our anxieties, and pours more garbage on our incomplete self-image to support the incomplete self-image and cause us to succumb to our own self-destruction.

You made the choice when you left the oversoul force. You made the choice to come into physical dimension, to experience certain associations, certain opportunities. And every association has its good side and its bad side. There are two sides to every coin, and it is up to us to balance out the bad side with the good side and the good side with the bad side. We need to see both and then move in a balanced sense into the reproductions of the creation of our vision of ourselves. There is no way around it, there is no way out of it. That's exactly where life is going to take you. And, individuals who are dealing with this "right to die," if they truly wanted to die, they would die. What they want is for someone else to administer the sting of death to them so that it cannot be called suicide.

Increasing sales through attraction

Seeker: I have a sales demonstration tomorrow, and I have demonstrations next week. After these demonstrations, I am exhausted because of all the people that come up and talk to me.

Jordan: Do you know why? Because you don't have one hundred percent faith in your product. You're trying to convince potential buyers that your product is the best for them. When you cease to try to convince them, and you believe you are doing them a service by sharing what you found to be a very worthwhile product, then by the *law of attraction* you will increase your sales a thousand percent.

Everybody has sensors, and what you project determines what you are going to attract. The reason I'm such a fine teacher is because I believe, through experience, that what I am teaching you works. I not only believe it, I know it. I live it, and I am a living example of it. So when I speak to you and I teach you, I'm teaching you on more than one level. I'm teaching you on three levels. It's not just the words that stimulate your intellectual mind, it's also the body language that stimulates your subconscious mind and it's the aura vibration that comes from the voice that stimulates all of your sensors. And you know it's true because it's carried across.

Which laws help us to utilize our guiding forces more completely?

Seeker: Impressions from my guiding forces come so fast that I have trouble grasping the first thought.

Jordan: That's right, and many people do. It takes training; it takes igniting the will of man to become the will of God. That's why you are taught to meditate and to do deep breathing. Through these physical disciplines you will eventually take control of the sensory and intellectual perceptive qualities, and they will hold onto those very fast impressions. But you must ignite the will, the desire and the overall goal. You must make the discernment instead of the judgment and the dissection.

That's why it all works together. In order to have better usage of your spirit forces you cannot be judgmental. You have to be aware that the *law of divine order* is in action and that the individuals who are utilizing your assistance, your expertise are getting exactly from life what they want from it. There is no bad, there is no good, it just is. If we concentrate on that, we'll be able to practice non-judgment and we'll be able to see everything working in its proper pattern.

Christ consciousness and the laws

Seeker: When Christ was asked how he was doing all the wonderful things he was doing, he said, "All things I have done, you can do." He also said, "It's the Father who is working through me." Does that mean that at some point in time, when we have reached the Christ consciousness, we will be able to bring the dead to life again?

Jordan: What is the actual concept of death? We bring the dead to life continuously when we educate. We awaken dead brain cells through stimulation. We awaken dead dimensions of the body and of the being through revealing new dimensions. So we are already bringing life to the dead. But you have forgotten a very important factor in that quotation because the whole quote says: All these things I have done you, too can do, **when you perform them in my name.** We cannot do it in the name of science, in the name of social acceptance, or in the name of personality aggrandizement. We must do it in the name of Jesus the Christ, the quintessence of unconditional love and understanding. Through that quintessence of unconditional love, we will see the *laws of cause and effect* and *divine order* in action. We will see the *law of non-judgment* being activated from within us as we confront the blemishes on the complexion of life and see them only as a source of information, not as an identification. We will expand in our self-acceptance, in our self-love and in our achievement of the self through the implantation of the principle of unconditional love and harmlessness.

We must practice harmlessness to the self first. When we are being harmless to the self, we can't do anything else but be harmless to all other creatures. But if we are going to perform those so called feats of phenomena, it's going to be because we do it in the name of Jesus the Christ.

We'll start by doing it in the names of our joy guide, our protector, our chemist, our inspirational teacher, in the name of the master influence that we've elected to serve under in our apprenticeship, because we are in apprenticeship.

In apprenticeship we do not attempt to usurp the master; we attempt to control the desire until we've perfected our abilities. When we do things in Christ's name, they are done as they are meant to be. But we can't have one bit of attachment to the good opinion of the recipient of the phenomena we are presenting. Christ also showed us the other side, because even his own disciples refused to perform the healing arts in his name, and they failed. They were too concerned about proving the healing arts. Because they didn't believe in the healing arts, the blind didn't see, the lame didn't walk, and the afflicted were still afflicted. It's very essential that we recognize the holy of holies that exists within us and activate that, certainly not this temporal identity.

Do you know why the practitioners of theosophy haven't done materialization? They started to interpret Blavatsky's teachings instead of following them. Do you know why the phenomena of trumpet levitation, apportation and materialization are dead except to a very few mediums who still do it? It's because everybody wishes to interpret them instead of simply to follow what made them.

Christ said: That which you do in my name—

We must step out of this shell, because this personality has a very limited understanding. We want to adopt a more harmless attitude; adopt another form of protection instead of all of our judgments and violence. We want to adopt a form of protection more in conjunction with nature and its natural force. We recognize the necessity of balanced chemistry, of the well-being of the body, and of the inspiration and mastery over the personality, with all of our desires to be seen as God. We are it, but there is a chain of command that we must follow in order to achieve it and express it in his name. That means we must become unconditional love. We must be prepared, in this physical personality form, to experience rejection from our parents, our students, our co-workers without having it cause us to doubt our purpose and intent. We don't need to look for proofs because we are the proof.

Potpourri

Seeker: Do we need to use enough discipline to break through the lower astral to tap into divine order so that we may clear up the thoughts that are left there? (Jordan: Of course.) In other words, when we create a vortex to cause and effect and we recognize all that is there, what do we do with it?

Jordan: You start working with it on a day-to-day basis. You have already found the avenue. I've already talked about self-discipline, self-motivation and self-projection. Isn't that exactly what yoga, Tai Chi, mind dynamics,

Catholicism, Judaism, Mohammedanism, Confucianism and Tibetanism do? These tools give you an avenue by which to discipline, motivate and project yourself. You don't do it by self-indulgence. Indulgence keeps you in the *law of compensation,* and when you reap the pain and the misery, that's when you usually come searching for an avenue by which to discipline yourself. Compensation gives you every tool that you need.

Seeker: When we're working on the frequency of divine order, everything is perfect?

Jordan: That's right. It's only your view of it that makes it imperfect. The Bible tells us that we are made and created in the image of God, that God is our Father. The Bible, the Bhagavad-Gita, the Koran, the Torah, and so forth, tell us that as long as we live in accordance with the laws that have been set down, which are basically the Ten Commandments, we will indeed control everything that happens in our lives. Divine order says that this planet is absolutely pure with everything on it. The impurity is how we comprehend it. The big problem is that man comprehends things in a very, very distorted view. Through my experience I have learned that the most devastating factors in my life have proven to be the *law of cause and effect* in action, allowing me to move into a greater sense of awareness. But I had to pay the price for it in the physical dimension by how I viewed it. That's the *law of compensation.*

Seeker: The words good and evil are coming to mind. In working with divine order and that everything is perfect, how are you able to deal with those concepts? Or are they man-made concepts?

Jordan: Those are man's concepts.

Seeker: Let's say killing people, or the act itself.

Jordan: There's a little book I would like you to read. It's called the *Thirteen Commandments* and it's written by J. Sig Paulson. Don't we kill each other by our negative thoughts, our judgments, our evaluations, our discernments? You mean physical war? Physical war is involved with the *law of compensation*. Physical war doesn't manifest until we've already killed one another by our thoughts, attitudes and actions. Then it becomes a physical representation. How many times have you thought that you would like to kill someone because he didn't meet your expectations, because he didn't do exactly what you wanted him to do? As a result wars become effective. You certainly are not going to blame a government or a political regime for what you yourself are doing, are you?

Look at yourself in your job and how you hate your boss. You absolutely kill him with your thoughts and your words. You talk about him in the most negative of ways.

Look at the associations that you've made. You speak about them in a negative way, and you kill a particular person's freedom of identity simply because she doesn't comprehend and understand what you're trying to manifest in your life.

Please don't be so ignorant that you don't believe that you create the wars. The wars are a reflection of your own hatred and self-hatred. There have been such wars fought in the name of righteousness and religion.

You can't believe that wars come under the *law of compensation?* Scriptures say: Remove the beam from your own eyes first before you try to remove it from your brother's eyes. What is that telling you? Wars are the *law of compensation* in action.

Seeker: Are you saying that divine order does not always exist, that we work through the other laws to get to divine order?

Jordan: I am saying that divine order is in action, we don't recognize its existence.

Seeker: You said that we kill one another mentally and emotionally and it then becomes physical in war.

I wonder, can we say that that's divine order?

Jordan: Divine order is, that perfection is, if we could recognize it. I think the problem is in recognizing it. I, as a clairvoyant, a psychic, a healer, must look at all of your outer manifestations and realize that they are good. I can't judge them, I can discern them. If I realize that they are good, I can energize greater good into them. But if I judge them as being a negative, then unfortunately I only energize a greater negative. Your discomforts and diseases are the very tools that will bring you to a greater sense of spiritual direction, to a greater sense of spiritual enlightenment, and the *laws of compensation* and *cause and effect* then become an action.

If I, as a reader or a healer, make a judgment because somebody is raping young children, then I unfortunately only energize the negative, as opposed to being able to express the positive. And the positive exists in the worst criminal. Psychology says that even the worst criminals will find a special place in their heart for something. Perhaps it will be an animal, perhaps it will be their mother, perhaps it will be something else. They have the milk and honey in their being, it needs to be brought out. You go through life making absolute concrete judgments that something is false and something else is true, which then only intensifies the *law of cause and effect*.

Ultimately, when you realize that everything is in divine order, you are able to perform in a balanced sense through all situations, and to learn the lesson from the *law of cause and effect* in action. If I taught you that the *law of cause and effect* denotes an imbalance in your perceptions and your awareness, which then represents karma, and it's the lower astral plane, then the *law of divine order* must be the higher astral plane. Then it certainly frees you from all of the limitations of this earthly situation. It's just your willingness to look at the *laws of cause and effect* and *compensation* and to redirect your thinking. Why has Jose Silva spent so much time to do his mind control and mind dynamics, except to give people the option to control their thinking, their actions and their words and to bring about the *law of compensation,* which frees them from money problems.

For example: If this man wouldn't have money problems all the time, he would be here studying with me and following his spiritual evolution. But he is being held by money problems, which is the *law of compensation.* Then we have the *law of cause and effect.* Perhaps his thinking is out of balance. Perhaps his spiritual desire is to study with me, but his physical desire is to make his mate happy and to do everything to prove what a wonderful man he is to her. She thinks she had three or four bad men, even though she created them because she is no easy person to live with. Anyway, you don't get to the law until you form the vortex. And that comes through a desire that has been brought about through the *law of compensation.*

After all, would she be here this weekend if her boyfriend hadn't left her? Isn't she concerned as to whether he will be back and if they are truly going to get married? That's the *law of compensation* for all of her doubts, fears, anxieties and her feelings. Why doesn't she have the perfect mate around her? She is the one who drives him away, yet she blames everybody else. Once she gets him, she has to deal with the *laws of compensation* and *cause and effect.* And then, eventually, she has to get to the *law of divine order.*

As you eventually see things in perfect order, you'll see that each individual must move through his or her own choices according to the *law of cause and effect.* I as a teacher may scold you occasionally and say, "What are you doing to yourself?" But I have learned over the years to step back and let you do what you want to do. Because you will ultimately find the high peak of the avenue, this lifetime or the next lifetime.

You will only compound what's in that lifetime. You are the creator of everything that you experience. For example: He has pushed his job away, and as soon as he looks at it, he can decide to do something about it. As long as he blames his job officials, he gives the power to someone else. Each and every one of you have pushed away what you wanted, and you are getting, in the *law of compensation,* exactly what you say and exactly what you know you are worthy of.

When you are dealing with the *law of cause and effect,* there are a certain amount of obstacles that are brought about by misbehaviors and misconduct from a past lifetime. When you create the vortex by understanding what you are experiencing in the physical realm, in the *law of compensation,* and you begin to control it, that's when money, emotional situations and educational situations all work out. But your problem is that you guess too much and you don't commit yourself. How do you know that your lover isn't going through such emotional problems that if you marry him now, you won't divorce him in six months?

Seeker: I know that we compound karma, but if everything is in divine order, is then any lifetime wasted?

Jordan: Yes, many of us waste a lot of time on our sojourn. How much energy do you put into negative thinking, into negative proclamation?

For example, a young man called me yesterday to tell me he didn't have any money. He wanted to come and study with me, but because he couldn't afford it he wouldn't see me until he could afford it. That's negative thinking. How much time do you put into analyzing your husband? How much time do you put into feeling sorry for yourself because he doesn't meet all of your expectations? How much time do you put into feeling sorry for yourself because you haven't gotten everything that you want, when you don't feel worthy of it in the first place? The only reason that

you are into cause and effect is because you are following a discipline, and you study with me. Stop and
think what the *law of compensation* is bringing about.
Your husband is the way he is because you think of
him that way. Your life is the way it is because you
think of it that way. If you would put a positive thought
into action, you would bring it into balance.

Seeker: Would you say that meditation moves us from compensation to divine order?

Jordan: It certainly can, as you move through the steps. But
you can't skip frequencies, you must move through
them. That's why many of our clairvoyants read for
themselves when they read for other people, and the
people in the audience know that the clairvoyants are
reading for themselves, because it is easy for them to
see. It's similar to when you read for somebody and
you thought, "My God, I'm reading for myself. I'm
actually educating myself." I have done it, and I'm
sure that some of you have done it.

Seeker: At that point you're attracting people with the same
situations?

Jordan: Yes, of course. The only thing that you're not putting
into action is the *law of divine order,* because you don't
understand it. You are still seeing things as a negative
and a positive.

Seeker: So when you're vacillating freely, you attract everyone?

Jordan: Of course. You will be attracting all manner of frequencies of individuals, but your sustaining factor will
be the *law of divine order.*

Seeker: How do we create the vortex between cause and effect and divine order?

Jordan: Do you want to know what it takes? It takes faith,
the one commodity most people don't have. That's a
mental discipline. Faith is the belief that all things
will be as you want them to be if you put forth one
hundred percent of your effort. The reason you don't
have faith is because you are not willing to put one

hundred percent of your effort into it.

Seeker: Under the definition of faith, would you define it as one hundred percent effort?

Jordan: Mental, emotional and physical effort. How can you be giving one hundred percent when your mind and your emotions are wandering some place else? I'll tell you what I was told. Until you eat it, drink it, sleep it, and live it 24 hours a day, you don't want it. When the *law of compensation* works, it brings you to a point where you do eat it, drink it, sleep it and live it. Then you want it. Up until that point you are just flirting with the vortex between the *laws of cause and effect* and *compensation*, and your life bespeaks it.

When you're tired and exhausted, that means you're flirting between the *laws of cause and effect* and *compensation*, and you haven't achieved the *law of divine order*, recognizing that all things are because they are meant to be, and that there is good that will come out of all of that which is transpiring in the physical dimension.

But many healers view the disorder instead of the good that can come from the disorder. It's the same thing when you generate money in your life. You're tired of being poor and dealing with all the poverty and all the things you lack. You stop feeling so ultimately good because you're experiencing all of these lacks and depressions, and you accept the responsibility for using your money wisely and in balance. Then all of a sudden you find that more money comes to you. Maybe you get your job changed. You've released the agitation caused by the so-called Pilate of limitation which is the *law of compensation* in action.

Faith is putting one hundred percent effort into all aspects. In order to get anything, you have to know you are entitled to it and know you are worthy of it. And you have to apply faith to attract and manifest it through the *laws of compensation* and *cause and effect*. Sometimes the things we think we want on the physical earth plane are deterred, or de-layed from manifesting because we are working through the *law of cause and effect,* which is also called karma and dharma. Faith is one hundred percent ef-fort because you get the *law of compensation* on a mo-ment-to-moment basis. It is in action right now, this minute. You're being compensated for either the bal-anced or the unbalanced effort that you are putting out, and your life shows it. If you are contented, happy, and secure in your growth, you are being compen-sated for your effort and your efforts show that you're balanced. When you are balanced, and you have cre-ated that balance to get the insight into your past associations, you are sometimes denied what you think you need and want instantaneously in life because you are moving into this frequency of the *law of cause and effect,* which deals with your karma and dharma. That means, before you can physically enjoy the situ-ation that you want and desire in your life, you must bring about a balance to this lower astral plane where you have left your unbalanced thoughts, attitudes, actions and words not just from this lifetime, but from many lifetimes. And, these thoughts, attitudes, actions and words are effective, active and creative in your life. You have to clean up all the garbage before you can get to the higher astral plane, and the higher as-tral plane is in divine order. That's where you see ev-erything working in its whole picture form; and you are not hung up by physically personalized energy identities.

Seeker: Does the soul mate come from divine order or like attracts like?

Jordan: The soul mate comes from like attracts like.

Seeker: Those laws are still tied in with the *law of compensa-tion?*

Jordan: Of course, because you haven't moved from that in-termediary or middle plane where you transmute your physical dense identity via the ultraviolet ray into your spiritual purpose. All of those laws are intertwined, and they become unified in oneness, as does everything on all the planes.

Seeker: We can also create on another level, not just on this physical earth plane?

Jordan: Anything can manifest in the astral dimensions by the power and the energy you give to it through thoughts, physical actions and emotional generation. After all, just fear something will be taken away from you and see how fast it's taken away from you. Just feel as though you're not giving one hundred percent to something and see how fast someone recognizes it, and tells you that you're not giving one hundred percent.

Seeker: What about thoughts?

Jordan: They are all manifesting in the *law of compensation.* That's why I made a point of telling you that once you have created a vortex from the *law of compensation,* which is in the physical earth plane, and you have seen a little bit of the *law of cause and effect,* and you have learned about your destiny from a medium, or you've found from a seer some of the spiritual forces that work with you and how they can assist you, then you really compound the *law of compensation.* Because you ultimately compound the intensity of the actions that you release in the physical earth plane. These bring about all of the physical and mental illnesses and all of the emotional distortions until you learn to deal with the *law of compensation* by recognizing what is in front of you and then letting God's will be done.

Seeker: In order to move into like attracts like, do I need to work on all three levels?

Jordan: You need to work on all three levels. You create a vortex through your desire and your self-discipline, and you begin to eradicate the karmic indebtedness with those individuals in your association.

The thing you don't realize and haven't accepted is that all of you, even those people who came from out of town, are here because you have a karmic tie that goes into the *law of cause and effect.* There is something for you to do here, and each time you avail yourself to the completion of this particular something, you open up the door for greater compensation to be manifested in your physical life.

I heard someone say, "The more I teach the more I find that my business improves, because I teach myself." That's the *law of compensation* in action. As a result you see in the physical dimension a compensation or a reward for your entrance into the clearing up of the imbalance in the lower astral planes. But as long as you only surround yourselves with your own physical, emotional and mental desires, you can't get into the lower astral planes. Then you are only frightened and manipulated by them, and you don't get rid of the imbalances. So you have to meet them in the physical dimension.

Seeker: When you're giving a reading to a person and you're discerning that a person has negative feelings about something—

Jordan: Every negative feeling has a basis of self-awareness behind it. And an individual must be able to take the negative feeling out, look at it, and decide to do something about it. It's like preparing yourself to be a salesman. If you have negative feelings about the product you are selling, then you transmit those negative feelings to the client that you are selling to. You must come to grips with the fact that you are actually providing a client with a beautiful service that he couldn't get anywhere else. Well perhaps he could, but you are offering him the greatest opportunity, which means that it is all in divine order. Then you come into the *law of cause and effect,* which means dharma and karma, and you realize that your associations are primarily based on the fact that you do have past life involvement. Very few of you are aware of what that involvement is, and whether it's balanced or unbalanced, but you know that divine order will prevail. So you can continue to respond and react as you do and as you must, knowing that divine order will prevail. When you have concluded that karmic association, the ties will sever. You will go your separate ways with great love, great harmony and great peace. There will be no need to come back and face them in another lifetime. I truly believe all of you are hoping to bring your life into a sense of balance, where you can leave this dimension, this kindergarten of the earth plane, and move into the other spheres of your associations.

Quite honestly, you will meet each other at various different times under various different circumstances and certainly in various different molecular structures, but your purpose is to make sure that you are balanced with one another and you do not act as a limitation to anyone who is indeed attempting to follow their own spiritual evolutionary pathway. That's why I have told Jane to stop worrying about her lover and to know that he will be coming back to her. She should give him the space and the freedom to deal with the *law of compensation* on the physical earth plane, because she doesn't want to deal with it while he is dealing with it. That's been her choice. Her only purpose should be to prepare herself to be the most balanced and the most aware when he is ready to come back and commit himself, as she knows he should and must. That's moving from the *laws of divine order, cause and effect*, and *like attracts like* to the *law of compensation.*

Seeker: In discussions, isn't telling people the truth sometimes in divine order?

Jordan: Sure. Tell them the truth. Don't cover up for them and don't try to win their approval. Come to a point inside yourself where you know it's divine order. It doesn't matter what my karmic association is with you, I don't want to control you. I would much rather you control yourself. I can say that to all of you because it doesn't matter to me what you do with your lives. I'm financially secure, emotionally secure and spiritually secure. So I can tell you the truth because I don't need you. When we think we need each other, we get caught up in these *laws of cause and effect* and *compensation*. I present myself most honestly and most totally and I say, "Here it is, kids. I really don't need you. If you want what I've got, then come and do what I've done to get it," which means, divine order and like attracts like is in action. I can tell you the truth because I'm so secure. If I were insecure, I would be saying, "Oh, you're so wonderful. I can help you do this, I can help you do that." I can't help you to do anything. You have to do it all on your own. You don't have to like me. I don't care if you like me because I like me.

I'm able to do those things because I love my students and I know what they are capable of doing. Why should I flatter them? Why should I tell them that they are something that they know they are not? I don't need their money.

All my life I thought it would be my karma to build a center. But in my heart I now realize that the center existed. So I found a sense of peace in the knowledge that I didn't have to build a center, not in a physical sense, because I found my center in my heart. That was moving through the laws to the other dimensions of them. I can be totally honest with anyone that comes and studies with me because I don't worry about what he or she may bring or not bring to the center. That takes us beyond the *law of like attracts like.*

Seeker: What about hands and faces I sometimes see in meditation? Do I have to leave that behind in order to move into the higher astral realm?

Jordan: All of those things that many of you see in the beginning of your meditations, such as eyes, faces, hands reaching up to hold you, and things of that nature will attract your attention. This is what we are most deliberately trying to bring into balance, because it's the blockade that prohibits us from moving into divine order, which is the higher astral realm. In the higher astral realm we see everything as perfect, as having its purpose, even the most terrible things that are taking place in the world at this point in time and the rebalancing of the earth population by those individuals who are dying and going to another place.

We have such a problem with transition because, truthfully, we don't always recognize that there is evolution that takes place on a day-to-day basis.

It doesn't matter whether the real true identity of yourself associates with me in this lifetime or in another lifetime. It is really your choice. It is immaterial as to how you got turned on to me. I just know what my job is, and I'm going to do my job to the best I can. Then you deal with it as you choose to, which then brings you back down in that basic order. When we get to these frequencies, it is because we opened and created the vortex between each frequency. When we merge a lower frequency into a higher frequency, we are getting sensitive awareness about people that we work with or are in association with. That simply means that it is accelerated from the point of the *law of compensation,* and that's the hardest one we deal with because we want to abort it.

Scripturally I can prove that to you because all of us at various times appear to be Christ standing before Pilate, whether that's the emotional Pilate, the intellectual Pilate, the monetary Pilate. We stand before Pilate and we give him the power to crucify us. But if we were like Christ and we would say, "You have no power over me unless it was in this particular frequency of divine order," then we would have control over the Pilates in our lives. We have to have such a basic concept. By viewing what we have done in our lives and feeling good about ourselves, we can look at the Pilate or compensation and say, "You have no power over me. It isn't that I don't accept you, but you just don't have the power over me." It's only what we give him, and we have to accept the fact that we have given it.

A final thought

We must know ourselves, accept ourselves, not indulge and deny ourselves; and we must work with these laws. The exterior is a compensation for our interior, so we don't fool anybody. If the natural laws are supposed to bring into our lives the opportunity to create the future of unity, harmony, love, prosperity, and health that we are entitled to live with, then we're going to have to be more masterful in our projections, interpretations and communications. We must stop making excuses, justifications and explanations, all of which deny our Godself, our child, our man, our woman and our spirit. Instead we want to select when, how and why we activate these selves and what they are supposed to bring about.

It doesn't take a great intellect to be able to see the natural laws working in our life right now. It does take people who want to give up their excuse-making and want to take their power back into their own hands, away from mystical icons or unknown influences that direct their intellect, their choices, their attitudes. It is their choices and their attitudes that bring about their undeniable compensations. Once we see, experience and live with our compensations, we cannot continue to deny that we must do something about them. We cannot give away to someone else the cause that has brought about the effect that we are living under.

We are the scales of perfection and imperfection. There in the middle we stand in perfect wisdom and illumination. It's only when we are attached to our imperfection that we reflect imperfect images. It's when we are only attached to our perfection, to our sainthood, that we reflect distorted images. But when we bring together our perfection and imperfection we reflect perfectly balanced, illuminated wisdom.

About the author

Rev. Ralph D. Jordan, DD, was born in Chicago, educated in traditional religion and metaphysical philosophies. Rev. Jordan holds ministerial and doctoral degrees from several associations. He met Hugh Lynn Cayce, the son of Edgar Cayce at the age of 17 and spent some time in discussion with him. Around the same time, in Chicago, Arthur Ford permitted Ralph to serve as his companion and nurse during the last weeks of his life, sharing much of what he had achieved in his life.

Rev. Jordan has studied Judaism, Catholicism and has been active in Protestantism. He is knowledgeable in the Islamic faith, the Tibetan faith and yoga. He has been a chela of Paramahansa Yogananda, is a Kriya initiate and past president of what was the second largest spiritualist camp in the United States.

He has established drug rehabilitation programs recognized by State government agencies. In the mid-60s, he was tested for his psychic abilities by scientific organizations dedicated to the research of phenomena. In 1974, he was tested by the Spiritualist Frontiers Fellowship Association. He was counselor for

U.S. government personnel and has worked in conjunction with Olaf Johnson, the mind connector to the first astronaut in space. Rev. Jordan is also founder and spiritual advisor of many spiritual organizations on the U.S. mainland, in Hawaii and Europe. He has been an internationally renowned teacher, lecturer, clairvoyant counselor, minister and physical phenomena medium for more than 35 years. He is one of the few active blindfold billet, apportation, trumpet levitation and materialization mediums.

Also by Ralph D. Jordan:

Psychic Counselor's Handbook
Ethics, Tools, and Techniques

In this masterful work, Ralph D. Jordan, gifted psychic counselor, shares a lifetime of insights into the successful conduct of a counseling practice as taught in his classes.

- What are the counselor's obligations to the client?
- When should you withhold unpleasant information?
- How does the counselor avoid becoming "vested" in a client?
- What should be the counselor's true purpose in a session?
- How do you prepare for a client?
- How do you counsel bereaved relatives?
- What if the client makes sexual advances?
- How do you discern a client's real motives in coming to you?
- What if you can't give the client what he or she needs?
- How do you know if you're trying to impress a client?
- What do you do when a client refuses to take responsibility?

No healer or counselor should be without this invaluable information.

Ask for ISBN 0-9667683-0-2.

You may obtain this book from any fine bookstore, online bookseller, or you may use the order form on the following page.

I f you liked this book, and would like to pass one on to someone else or if you would like to order *Psychic Counselor's Handbook*, please check with your local bookstore, online bookseller,
or use this form:

Name _____

Address _____

City _____ State _____ Zip _____

Tel. _____ Fax _____

e-mail _____

Payment by: ☐ Check   ☐ Money Order   ☐ Credit Card

Credit Card Number: _____

Expiration Date: _____

Check which: ☐ MasterCard   ☐ Visa

Discovering the Natural Laws
that govern the Universe _____ copies @ $14.95 ea. $ _____

Psychic Counselor's Handbook
Ethics, Tools, and Techniques _____ copies @ $14.95 ea. $ _____

Hawaii residents, please add applicable sales tax $ _____

Shipping: $3.50/first copy;
$2.00 each additional copy $ _____

Total enclosed, or charge my credit card (above) $ _____

For more than 5 copies, please contact the publisher for quantity
rates. Send completed order form and your payment to:

> **Inner Perceptions, Inc.**
> **P. O. Box 2652**
> **Kailua-Kona, HI 96745**
> **Phone/Fax: 808-325-5268**
> **email: nich@gte.net**

or order via our Web Site at **www.innerperceptions.com**
Visa and MasterCard accepted.

International shipping is extra. Please contact us for the shipping
rates to your location, if outside the United States.